MASSACHUSETTS
HIKING

MASSACHUSETTS
HIKING

First Edition

Michael Lanza

AVALON
TRAVEL

FOGHORN OUTDOORS MASSACHUSETTS HIKING

First Edition

Michael Lanza

Printing History
1st edition—April 2005
5 4 3 2 1

Avalon Travel Publishing
An Imprint of
Avalon Publishing Group, Inc.

AVALON
publishing group incorporated

ISBN: 1-56691-936-3
ISSN: 1553-6122

Editor and Series Manager: Ellie Behrstock
Acquisitions Editor: Rebecca Browning
Copy Editors: Donna Leverenz
Graphics Coordinator: Deborah Dutcher
Production Coordinator: Darren Alessi
Cover and Interior Designer: Darren Alessi
Map Editors: Olivia Solís, Naomi Adler Dancis, Kat Smith, Kevin Anglin
Cartographers: Kat Kalamaras, Mike Morgenfeld

Front cover photo: Mount Katahdin, Baxter State Park, © Phil Schermeister/Network Aspen

Printed in the USA by Malloy, Inc.

About the Author

An avid four-season hiker, backpacker, climber, skier, and road and mountain biker, Michael Lanza first fell in love with hiking and the outdoors in New Hampshire's White Mountains 20 years ago. For years, he spent weekend after weekend hiking in the Whites, then branched out all over New England. During the year that he researched and wrote the first edition of *Foghorn Outdoors New England Hiking,* he figures he hiked 1,200 miles, covering all six New England states. He's now hiked and climbed extensively in the West and Northeast and as far afield as Nepal, but still returns regularly to New England to hike.

Michael is the Northwest Editor of *Backpacker* magazine and writes a monthly column and other articles for *AMC Outdoors* magazine. His work has also appeared in *National Geographic Adventure, Outside,* and other publications. He is also the author of *Foghorn Outdoors New England Hiking, Foghorn Outdoors Maine Hiking, Foghorn Outdoors New Hampshire Hiking,* and *Foghorn Outdoors Vermont Hiking.*

During the mid-1990s Michael syndicated a weekly column about outdoor activities in about 20 daily newspapers throughout New England and co-hosted a call-in show about the outdoors on New Hampshire Public Radio. A native of Leominster, Massachusetts, Michael has a B.S. in photojournalism from Syracuse University and spent 10 years as a reporter and editor at various Massachusetts and New Hampshire newspapers. When he's not hiking the trails of New England, he can be found in Boise, Idaho, with his wife, Penny Beach, and their son, Nate, and daughter, Alex.

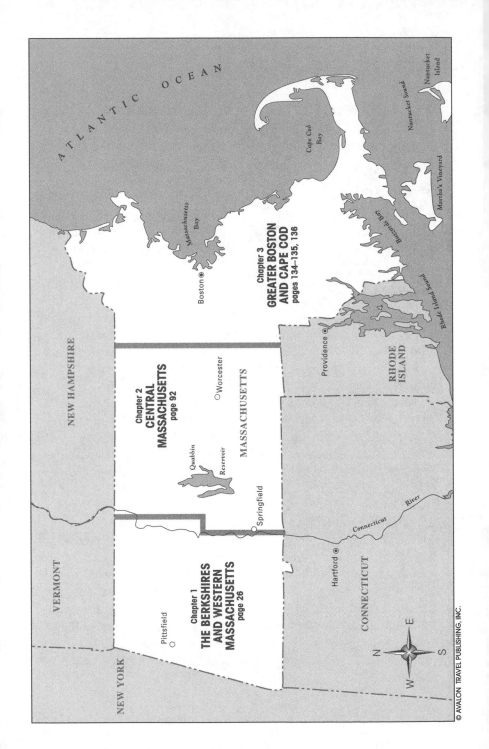

© AVALON TRAVEL PUBLISHING, INC.

Contents

Including:
- Bash Bish Falls State Park
- Beartown State Forest
- D.A.R. State Forest
- Granville State Forest
- Mohawk Trail State Forest
- Mount Greylock State Reservation
- Mount Sugarloaf State Reservation
- Mount Tom State Reservation
- Mount Washington State Forest
- Savoy Mountain State Forest

Including:
- Douglas State Forest
- Leominster State Forest
- Purgatory Chasm State Reservation
- Skinner State Park
- Wachusett Mountain State Reservation
- Willard Brook State Forest

Including:
- Blue Hills Reservation
- Boxford State Forest
- Bradley Palmer State Park
- Cape Cod National Seashore
- Caratunk Wildlife Refuge
- Charles River Reservation
- Great Meadows National Wildlife Refuge

- Halibut Point State Park and Reservation
- Maudslay State Park
- Middlesex Fells Reservation
- Sandy Point State Reservation
- Upton State Forest
- Walden Pond State Park Reservation

 Our Commitment

We are committed to making *Foghorn Outdoors Massachusetts Hiking* the most accurate and enjoyable hiking guide to the state. With this first edition you can rest assured that every hiking trail in this book has been carefully reviewed and is accompanied by the most up-to-date information. Be aware that with the passing of time some of the fees listed herein may have changed, and trails may have closed unexpectedly. If you have a specific need or concern, it's best to call the location ahead of time.

If you would like to comment on the book, whether it's to suggest a trail we overlooked, or to let us know about any noteworthy experience—good or bad—that occurred while using *Foghorn Outdoors Massachusetts Hiking* as your guide, we would appreciate hearing from you. Please address correspondence to:

Foghorn Outdoors Massachusetts Hiking, first edition
Avalon Travel Publishing
1400 65th Street, Suite 250
Emeryville, CA 94608

email: atpfeedback@avalonpub.com
If you send us an email, please put "Massachusetts Hiking" in the subject line.

How to Use This Book

Foghorn Outdoors Massachusetts Hiking is divided into three chapters, based on major regions of the state. Regional maps show the location of all the hikes in that chapter.

>**For The Berkshires and Western Massachusetts:** see
>   pages 23–88
>**For Central Massachusetts:** see pages 89–129
>**For Greater Boston and Cape Cod:** see pages 131–191

There are two ways to search for the perfect hike:
1. If you know the name of the specific trail you want to hike, or the name of the surrounding geographical area or nearby feature (town, national or state park, or forest, mountain, lake, river, etc.), look it up in the index and turn to the corresponding page.
2. If you want to find out about hiking possibilities in a particular part of the state, turn to the map at the beginning of that chapter. You can then determine the area where you would like to hike and identify which hikes are available; then turn to the corresponding numbers for those hikes in the chapter.

Trail Names, Distances, and Times
Each trail in this book has a number, name, mileage information, and estimated completion time. The trail's number allows you to find it easily on the corresponding chapter map. The name is either the actual trail name (as listed on signposts and maps) or a name I've given to a series of trails or a loop trail. In the latter cases, the name is taken from the major destination or focal point of the hike.

Most mileage listings are precise, though a few are very good estimates. All mileages and approximate times refer to round-trip travel unless specifically noted as one-way. In the case of one-way hikes, a car or bike shuttle is advised.

The estimated time is based on how long I feel an average adult in moderate physical condition would take to complete the hike. Actual times can vary widely, especially on longer hikes.

What the Ratings Mean

Every hike in this book has been rated on a scale of 1 to 10 for its overall quality and on a scale of 1 to 10 for difficulty.

The quality rating is based largely on scenic qualities, although it also takes into account how crowded a trail is and whether or not you see or hear civilization.

The difficulty rating is calculated based on the following scale:

10 —The hike entails all of the following qualities: climbs 3,000+ feet in elevation, covers at least seven miles, and has rugged and steep terrain with some exposure.

9 —The hike entails at least two of the following qualities: climbs 2,500+ feet in elevation, covers at least seven miles, and/or has rugged and steep terrain with some exposure.

8 —The hike entails one or more of the following qualities: climbs 2,000+ feet in elevation, covers at least seven miles, or has rugged and steep terrain with possible exposure.

7 —The hike entails at least two of the following qualities: climbs 1,500+ feet in elevation, covers at least five miles, and/or has steep and rugged sections.

6 —The hike entails one of the following qualities: climbs 1,500+ feet in elevation, covers at least five miles, or has steep and rugged sections.

5 —The hike covers at least four miles and either climbs 1,000+ feet in elevation or has steep, rugged sections.

4 —The hike entails one of the following qualities: climbs 1,000+ feet in elevation, covers at least four miles, or has steep, rugged sections.

3 —The hike has some hills—though not more than 1,000 feet of elevation gain—and covers at least three miles.

2 —The hike either has some hills—though not more than 1,000 feet of elevation gain—or covers at least three miles.

1 —The trail is relatively flat and less than three miles.

Hike Descriptions

The description for each listing is intended to give you some idea of what kind of terrain to expect, what you might see, and how to follow the hike from beginning to end. I've sometimes added a special note about the hike or a suggestion on how to combine it with a nearby hike or expand upon your outing in some other way.

There are a couple of terms used throughout the book that reflect the land usage history in the region. Forest roads are generally dirt or gravel roads maintained by the land manager and are typically not open to motor vehicles except those of the manager. Woods roads, or "old woods roads," are abandoned thoroughfares—many were formerly public routes between colonial communities—now heavily overgrown, but recognizable as a wide path. Their condition can vary greatly.

User Groups

I have designated a list of user groups permitted on each trail, including hikers, bicyclists, dogs, horses, hunters, cross-country skiers, snowshoers, and wheelchair users.

While this book is intended primarily as a hiking guide, it includes some trails that are mediocre hikes yet excellent mountain biking or cross-country skiing routes. The snowshoe reference is intended as a guide for beginners; experienced snowshoers know that many Massachusetts trails can be snowshoed in winter, but this book indicates when snowshoeing a trail may require advanced winter hiking skills. As always, the individual must make the final judgment regarding safety issues in winter.

Wheelchair accessibility is indicated when stated by the land or facility manager, but concerned persons should call to find out if their specific needs will be met.

The hunting reference is included to remind hikers to be aware of the hunting season when hiking, and that they may be sharing a trail with hunters, in which case they should take the necessary precautions (wearing a bright color, preferably fluorescent orange) to avoid an accident in the woods. Hunting is a popular sport in Massachusetts and throughout New England. The hunting season generally extends from fall into early winter. The state parks and forests offices can provide you with actual dates (see Resources in the back of the book for contact information).

Access and Fees
This section provides information on trail access, entrance fees, parking, and hours of operation.

Maps
Information on how to obtain maps for a trail and environs is provided for each hike listing. When several maps are mentioned, you might want to ask the seller about a map's detail, weather-proofness, range, and scale when deciding which one to obtain. Consider also which maps will cover other hikes that interest you. Prices are usually indicative of quality and detail. I've also listed the appropriate United States Geologic Survey (USGS) map or maps covering that area. Be advised that many USGS maps do not show trails or forest roads, and that trail locations may not be accurate if the map has not been updated recently. Massachusetts is covered by 7.5-by-15-minute series maps (1:25,000). An index map also covers Massachusetts/Connecticut/Rhode Island, showing the 7.5-minute and 15-minute maps.

See Resources in the back of the book for map sources. To order individual USGS maps or the New England index maps, write to USGS Map Sales, Federal Center, Box 25286, Denver, CO 80225.

Directions
This section provides mile-by-mile driving directions to the trailhead from the nearest major town.

Contact
Most of the hikes in this book list at least one contact agency, trail club, or organization for additional information. Many hikes will give you a sample of something bigger—a long-distance trail or public land. Use the contact information to explore beyond what is found in these pages. And remember to support the organizations listed here that maintain the trails you hike.

© MICHAEL LANZA

Author's Note

Dear fellow hiker,

I have a single black-and-white photograph from what was probably my first hike up a mountain. It shows two friends and me—young, dressed in flannel shirts and jeans—standing on a rocky New England summit. In the distance, clouds blot out much of the sky. The wind lifts our hair and fills our shirts; it appears to be a cool day in early autumn.

I no longer recall what peak we hiked, only that the hike had been the idea of one of my friends; I was tagging along on an outing that seemed like something I might enjoy. In fact, my recollection of the entire day amounts to little more than a lingering sense of the emotions it generated for me—kind of an artifact of memory, like an arrowhead dug up somewhere.

I was perhaps 18 or 20 years old, and standing on top of that little mountain struck me as quite possibly the most intense and wonderful thing I'd ever done.

Of course, at that age most people have limited experience with things intense and wonderful. But I found that as my fascination with high places grew, so did the inspiration that began on that first summit.

I have since done much hiking all over Massachusetts and the rest of New England and taken my thirst for that feeling to bigger mountains out West—hiking, backpacking, and climbing in the Sierra Nevada, the Cascades and Olympics, the Tetons and Wind River Range, the Rockies from Colorado to Alberta, and Alaska. My work allows me to spend many days and nights every year in wild country.

When asked to write *Foghorn Outdoors New England Hiking,* I realized I would spend a summer hiking trails I had not yet visited but which belong in a guide this comprehensive. While I expected to sorely miss the West, where I'd been spending summers hiking and climbing, instead I found myself enjoying a reunion of sorts with my hiking roots. I finally got to many places that had been on my checklist for some time. And, to my surprise, the hikes I relished most were those I had known the least about, those scattered trails that for various reasons attract relatively few hikers.

Foghorn Outdoors Massachusetts Hiking is the product of many days on the trail and a reflection of many personal memories. As you use it to explore Massachusetts' trails, I urge you to walk lightly, to do your part to help preserve these fragile places, and to venture beyond the popular, well-beaten paths to lesser-known destinations.

I also invite you to let me know about any inaccuracies by writing to my publisher, Avalon Travel Publishing, at the following address: Foghorn Outdoors Massachusetts Hiking, Avalon Travel Publishing, 1400 65th Street, Suite 250, Emeryville, CA 94608.

I hope this book helps you find the same kind of experiences I have enjoyed in these mountains and forests—to discover your own arrowhead.

—*Michael Lanza*

Massachusetts Overview

Massachusetts offers a great diversity of trails, from the rolling green hills of the Berkshires to the wonderful coastal hikes in the Cape Cod National Seashore. The Bay State also boasts one of the largest state park and forest systems in the country, with nearly 100 properties covering more than 270,000 acres—most of them crisscrossed by trails and old woods roads—and three long-distance trails bisecting the state north to south: 90 miles of the Appalachian Trail, the 117-mile Metacomet-Monadnock Trail, and the 92-mile Midstate Trail.

Western Massachusetts and the Berkshires are characterized by low, green hills rising abruptly from heavily wooded valleys. While these hikes are mostly in the woods, there's also a surprising abundance of views given the low elevations. Mount Greylock and the Riga Plateau stretch of the Appalachian Trail (AT) are probably the two best-known highlights—and deserve their popularity—but there are numerous other gems in these hills, like Monument Mountain, Mount Everett, Alander Mountain, and the Hubbard River Gorge.

Central Massachusetts harbors some of the quietest, least-trampled trails in the Bay State, many of them very scenic and enjoyable. Wachusett Mountain's distinctive profile dominates this landscape of low, wooded, rolling hills, but there are several other state lands that make great, uncrowded recreational destinations.

The Greater Boston and Cape Cod region has widely varied hiking. The wonderful trails of the Middlesex Fells and Blue Hills are tucked in amid the sprawling urban area, to various public lands scattered around the eastern part of the state, to the major destination of the Cape Cod National Seashore, where you can actually find quiet trails and beaches to escape from the madding crowds elsewhere on the Cape.

Perhaps the most famous hiking trail in the world, the Appalachian Trail (AT) runs 2,174 miles from Springer Mountain in Georgia to Mount Katahdin in Maine, along the spine of the Appalachian Mountains in 14 states.

About 90 miles of the Appalachian Trail pass through the Berkshires of western Massachusetts. Among the highlights of the Bay State's portion of the Appalachian Trail are the Riga Plateau—which extends into the very northwestern corner of Connecticut—and Mount Greylock.

A few hundred people hike the entire Appalachian Trail end to end every year, but countless thousands take shorter backpacking trips and day hikes somewhere along the Appalachian Trail. Well maintained by various hiking clubs that assume responsibility for different sections, the trail is well marked with signs and white blazes on trees and rocks, or cairns above treeline. Shelters and campsites are spaced out along the Appalachian Trail so that backpackers have choices of where to spend each night, but those shelters can fill up during the busy season of summer and early fall, especially on weekends.

The prime hiking season for the Appalachian Trail in western Massachusetts generally runs from May through October or even November—a longer season than in the higher-elevation mountains in northern New England.

Hiking Tips

Climate

With its highest hills arrayed in the western part of the state, and its terrain growing gentler and flatter moving toward the ocean, Massachusetts has some of the most varied hiking found in New England. But the varied character of hiking opportunities here also demands some basic knowledge of and preparation for hitting the trails.

The prime hiking season in Massachusetts stretches for several months from spring through fall, with the season's length depending on the region. September is often the best month for hiking, with dry, comfortable days, cool nights, and few bugs. Fall foliage colors peak anywhere from early to mid-October. The period from mid-October into November offers cool days, cold nights, no bugs, few people, and no snow.

The ocean generally keeps the coast a little warmer in winter and cooler in summer than inland areas. In general, summer high temperatures range from 60–90°F with lows from 50°F to the 70s or hotter. Days are often humid. July and August see occasional thunderstorms, but July through September are the driest months.

Black flies, or mayflies, emerge by late April or early May and pester hikers until late June or early July, while mosquitoes come out in late spring and dissipate (but do not disappear) by midsummer.

Along the Appalachian Trail in western Massachusetts, higher-elevation snow disappears and alpine wildflowers bloom in late spring; by late October, wintry winds start blowing. Spring trails are muddy and may hold snow in shaded pockets at the highest elevations. Winter conditions set in by December.

In the smaller hills and flatlands of central and eastern Massachusetts, the snow-free hiking season often begins by early spring and lasts into late autumn. Some of these trails are even occasionally free of snow during the winter, or offer opportunities for snowshoeing or cross-country skiing in woods protected from strong winds, with warmer temperatures than you'll find on the bigger peaks of northern New England. Seacoast trails

Cross-Country Skiing and Snowshoeing

Many hikes in this book are great for cross-country skiing or snowshoeing in winter. But added precaution is needed. Days are short and the temperature may start to plummet by mid-afternoon, so carry the right clothing and don't overestimate how far you can travel in winter. Depending on snow conditions and your own fitness level and experience with either snowshoes or skis, a winter outing can take much longer than anticipated—and certainly much longer than a trip of similar distance on groomed trails at a cross-country ski resort. Breaking your own trail through fresh snow can also be very exhausting—take turns leading, and conserve energy by following the leader's tracks, which also serve as a good trail to return on.

The proper clothing becomes essential in winter, especially the farther you wander from roads. Wear a base layer that wicks moisture from your skin and dries quickly (synthetics or wool, not cotton), middle layers that insulate and do not retain moisture, and a windproof shell that breathes well and is waterproof or water-resistant (the latter type of garment usually breathes much better than something that's completely waterproof). Size boots to fit over a thin, synthetic liner sock and a thicker, heavyweight synthetic-blend sock. For your hands, often the most versatile system consists of gloves and/or mittens that also can be layered, with an outer layer that's water- and windproof and preferably also breathable.

Most importantly, don't overdress: Remove layers if you're sweating heavily. Avoid becoming wet with perspiration, which can lead to you cooling too much. Drink plenty of fluids and eat snacks frequently to maintain your energy level; feeling tired or cold on a winter outing may be an indication of dehydration or hunger.

As long as you're safe, cautious, and aware, winter is a great time to explore New England's trails. Have fun out there.

rarely get snow, though they can get occasional heavy snowfall and be icy.

For more information about weather-related trail conditions, refer to the individual hike listings.

Basic Hiking Safety

Few of us would consider hiking a high-risk activity. But like any physical activity, it does pose certain risks, and it's up to us to minimize them. For starters, make sure your physical condition is adequate to your objective—the quickest route to injury is overextending either your skills or your physical abilities. You wouldn't

(F) First-Aid Checklist

Although you're probably at greater risk of injury while driving to the trail-head than you are on the trail, it's wise to carry a compact and lightweight first-aid kit for emergencies in the backcountry, where an ambulance and hospital are often hours, rather than minutes, away. Many are available at outdoor gear retailers. Or prepare your own first-aid kit with attention to the type of trip, the destination, and the needs of people hiking (for example, children or persons with medical conditions). Pack everything into a thick, clear plastic resealable bag. And remember, merely carrying a first-aid kit does not make you safe; knowing how to use what's in it does.

A basic first-aid kit consists of:

- ❑ 2 large cravats
- ❑ 2 large gauze pads
- ❑ 4 four-inch-square gauze pads
- ❑ 1 six-inch Ace bandage
- ❑ roll of one-inch athletic tape
- ❑ several one-inch adhesive bandages
- ❑ several alcohol wipes
- ❑ safety pins
- ❑ tube of povidone iodine ointment (for wound care)
- ❑ Moleskin or Spenco Second Skin (for blisters)
- ❑ knife or scissors
- ❑ paper and pencil
- ❑ aspirin or an anti-inflammatory medication
- ❑ SAM splint (a versatile and lightweight splinting device available at many drug stores)
- ❑ blank SOAP note form

presume that you could rock climb a 1,000-foot cliff if you've never climbed before; don't assume you're ready for one of the Bay State's hardest hikes if you've never—or not very recently—done anything nearly as difficult.

Build up your fitness level by gradually increasing your workouts and the length of your hikes. Beyond strengthening muscles, you must strengthen the soft connective tissue in joints like knees and ankles that are too easily strained and take weeks or months to heal from injury. Staying active in a variety of activities—hiking, running, bicycling, Nordic skiing, etc.—helps develop good overall fitness and decreases the likelihood of an overuse injury.

Most importantly, stretch muscles before and after a workout to reduce the chance of injury.

Massachusetts' most rugged trails—and even parts of its more moderate paths—can be rocky and steep. Uneven terrain is often a major contributor to falls resulting in serious, acute injury. Most of us have a fairly reliable self-preservation instinct—and you should trust it. If something strikes you as dangerous or beyond your abilities, don't try it, or simply wait until you think you're ready for it.

An injury far from a road also means it may be hours before the victim reaches a hospital. Basic training in wilderness first aid is beneficial to anyone who frequents the mountains, even recreational hikers. New England happens to have two highly respected sources for such training, and the basic course requires just one weekend. Contact SOLO (Conway, NH; 603/447-6711, website: www.solo schools.com) or Wilderness Medical Associates (Bryant Pond, ME; 888/945-3633, website: www.wildmed.com) for information.

Clothing and Gear

Much could be written about how to outfit oneself for hiking in Massachusetts, with its significant range of elevations and weather, huge seasonal temperature swings, and fairly wet climate. But in the simplest of terms, you should select your clothing and equipment based on:

- the season and the immediate weather forecast
- the amount of time you plan to be out (a couple of hours, a full day, more than one day)
- the distance you'll be wandering from major roads
- the elevation you will hike to
- the abilities of your hiking companions

At lower elevations amid the protection of trees or on a warm day, you may elect to bring no extra clothing for an hour-long outing, or no more than a light jacket for a few hours or more. The exception to this is in the Seacoast region, where hikes are more exposed to cool wind. But higher elevations, especially above tree line, get much colder than the valleys—about three degrees Fahrenheit per thousand feet—and winds can grow much stronger. Insulating layers, a jacket that protects against wind and precipitation, a warm hat, and gloves are always a good idea when climbing Massachusetts' highest hills.

The most important piece of gear may be well-fitting, comfortable, supportive shoes or boots. Finding the right footwear requires trying on various models and walking around in them in the store before deciding. Everyone's feet are different, and shoes or boots that feel great on your friend won't necessarily fit you well. Deciding how heavy your footwear should be depends on variables like how often you hike, whether you easily injure feet or ankles, and how much weight you'll carry. Generally, I recommend hiking in the most lightweight footwear that you find comfortable and adequately supportive.

Above all, use good judgment and proceed with caution. When you're not sure, take the extra layer of clothing, just in case.

Foot Care

At an Appalachian Mountain Club seminar on winter backpacking that I attended years ago, one instructor told us that, besides the brain, "Your feet are the most important part of your body." Hurt any other body part and you might conceivably still make it home under your own power. Hurt your feet, and you're in trouble.

Take care of your feet. Wear clean socks that wick moisture from your skin while staying dry. If you anticipate your socks getting wet from perspiration or water, bring extra socks; on a multiday trip, have dry socks for each day, or at least change socks every other day. Make sure your shoes or boots fit properly, are laced properly, and are broken in if they require it. Wear the appropriate footwear for the type of hiking you plan to do.

Whenever I stop for a short rest on the trail—even if only for a few minutes—I sit down, pull off my boots and socks, and let them and my feet dry out. When backpacking, wash your feet at the end of the day. If you feel any hot spots developing, intervene before they progress into blisters. A slightly red or tender hot spot can be protected from developing into a blister with an adhesive bandage, tape, or a square of moleskin.

If a blister has formed, clean the area around it thoroughly to avoid infection. Sterilize a needle or knife in a flame, then pop and

drain the blister to promote faster healing. Put an antiseptic ointment on the blister. Cut a piece of moleskin or Second Skin (both
of which have a soft side and a sticky side with a peel-off backing)
large enough to overlap the blistered area. Cut a hole as large as the
blister out of the center of the moleskin, then place the moleskin
over the blister so that the blister is visible through the hole. If done
properly, you should be able to walk without aggravating the blister.

Water and Food

Streams and brooks run everywhere in Massachusetts. If you're
out for more than a day in the backcountry, finding water is rarely
a problem (except on ridgetops and summits). But protozoans and
bacteria occur in backcountry water sources, and campers do not
always maintain an appropriate distance between their messes and
the stream. Assume you should always treat water from backcountry sources, whether by using a filter or iodine tablets, boiling, or
another proven method. Day hikers will usually find it more convenient to simply carry enough water from home for the hike.

Most of us require about two liters of water per day when we're
not active. Like any physical activity, hiking increases your body's
fluid needs by a factor of two or more. On a hot, sticky summer
day, or even on a cold, dry winter day (when the air draws moisture from your body even though you may not be perspiring),
you'll need even more water than you would on a cool autumn afternoon. A good rule of thumb for an all-day hike is two liters of
water per person, but that could even leave you mildly dehydrated,
so carry a third liter if you think you may need it. Dehydration
can lead to other, more serious problems, like heat exhaustion, hy-
pothermia, frostbite, and injury. If you're well hydrated, you will
urinate frequently and your urine will be clear. The darker your
urine, the greater your level of dehydration. If you feel thirsty, dehydration has already commenced. In short: Drink a lot.

Similarly, your body consumes a phenomenal amount of calories
walking up and down a mountain. Feed it frequently. Carbohy-
drates like bread, chocolate, dried fruit, fig bars, snack bars, fresh
vegetables, and energy bars provide a source of quick energy. Fats
contain about twice the calories per pound than carbs or protein,
and provide the slow-burning fuel that keeps you going all day and
warm through the night if you're sleeping outside; sate your need

for fats by eating cheese, chocolate, canned meats or fish, pepperoni, sausage, or nuts.

Animals
While the Massachusetts hills and forests have a variety of wildlife, including black bears and even the occasional moose (not to mention more rare species like wildcat and bald eagle), for the most part, you don't have to worry for your safety in the backcountry. In years of hiking, I've never encountered a bear on the trail, though I've seen scat and other signs of their presence.

Still, a few sensible precautions are in order. If you're camping in the backcountry, know how to hang or store your food properly to keep it from bears and smaller animals like mice, which are more likely to be a problem. If you're fortunate enough to see a moose or bear, you certainly should never approach either. These creatures are wild and unpredictable, and a moose can weigh several hundred pounds and put the hurt on a much smaller human.

The greatest danger posed by wildlife is that of hitting an animal while driving on dark back roads at night, which can wreck vehicles and injure people. At night, drive more slowly than you would during daylight.

Low-Impact Practices
Many Massachusetts trails receive heavy use, making it imperative that we all understand how to minimize our physical impact on the land. The nonprofit organization Leave No Trace (LNT) advocates a set of principles for low-impact backcountry use that are summarized in these basic guidelines:

- Plan ahead and prepare
- Travel and camp on durable surfaces
- Dispose of waste properly
- Leave what you find
- Minimize campfire impact
- Respect wildlife
- Be considerate of other visitors

Below are more-specific recommendations that apply to many backcountry areas:

Long-Distance Trails in Massachusetts

Besides a section of the Appalachian Trail, the Bay State boasts two "long trails" that are entirely, or almost entirely, within its borders. The Metacomet-Monadnock Trail bounces along the Holyoke Range and through the hills of north-central Massachusetts on its 117-mile course from the Massachusetts-Connecticut line near Agawam and Southwick to the summit of Mount Monadnock in Jaffrey, New Hampshire. The Midstate Trail extends 92 miles from Douglas, on the Rhode Island border, to the New Hampshire line in Ashburnham. Significant stretches of the Metacomet-Monadnock and Midstate trails are on private land, so be aware of and respect any closures.

- Choose a campsite at least 200 feet from trails and water sources, unless you're using a designated site. Make sure your site bears no evidence of your stay when you leave.
- Avoid building campfires; cook with a backpacking stove.
- Carry out everything you carry in.
- Do not leave any food behind, even buried, as animals will dig it up. Learn how to hang food appropriately to keep it from bears. Black bears have spread their range over much of New England in recent years, and problems have arisen in isolated backcountry areas where human use is heavy.
- Bury human waste beneath six inches of soil at least 200 feet from any water source. Burn and bury, or carry out, used toilet paper.
- Even biodegradable soap is harmful to the environment, so simply wash your cooking gear with water away from any streams or ponds.
- Avoid trails that are very muddy in spring; that's when they are most susceptible to erosion.
- And last but not least, know and follow any regulations for the area you will be visiting.

LNT offers more in-depth guidelines for low-impact camping and hiking on its website, www.lnt.org. You can also contact them by mail or phone: Leave No Trace Inc., P.O. Box 997, Boulder, CO 80306; 303/442-8222 or 800/332-4100, website: www.lnt.org.

Trail Etiquette

One of the great things about hiking—at least for as long as I've been hiking—has always been the quality of the people you meet on the trail. Hikers generally do not need an explanation of the value of courtesy, and I hope that will always ring true.

Personally, I yield the trail to others whether I'm going uphill or down. All trail users should yield to horses by stepping aside for the safety of everyone present. Likewise, horseback riders should, whenever possible, avoid situations where their animals are forced to push past hikers on very narrow trails. Mountain bikers should yield to hikers, announce their approach, and pass non-bikers slowly. During hunting season, non-hunters should wear blaze orange, or an equally bright, conspicuous color. Most of the hunters I meet are responsible and friendly and deserve like treatment.

Many of us enjoy the woods and mountains for the quiet, and we should keep that in mind on the trail, at summits, or back-country campsites. Many of us share the belief that things like cell phones, radios, CD players, and hand-held personal computers do not belong in the mountains; if you must use them, use discretion.

This region has seen some conflict between hikers and mountain bikers, but it's important to remember that solutions to those

---

 Hiking Blazes

New England's forests abound with blazes—slashes of paint on trees used to mark trails. Sometimes the color of blazes seems random and unrelated to other trails in the same area, but most major trails and trail systems are blazed consistently. The Appalachian Trail bears white blazes for its entire length, including its 90 miles within Massachusetts. Most side trails connecting to the Appalachian Trail are blazed with blue paint. Although not all trails are well blazed, popular and well-maintained trails usually are—you'll see a colored slash of paint at frequent intervals at about eye level on tree trunks. Double slashes are sometimes used to indicate a sharp turn in the trail. Trails are blazed in both directions, so whenever you suspect you may have lost the trail, turn around to see whether you can find a blaze facing in the opposite direction; if so, you'll know you're still on the trail.

Above tree line, trails may be marked either with blazes painted on rock or with cairns, which are piles of stone constructed at regular intervals.

---

issues are never reached through hostility and rudeness. Much more is accomplished when we begin from a foundation of mutual respect and courtesy. After all, we're all interested in preserving and enjoying our trails.

Large groups have a disproportionate impact on backcountry campsites and on the experience of other people. Be aware of and respect any restrictions on group size. Even where no regulation exists, keep your group size to no more than 10 people.

Dogs can create unnecessary friction in the backcountry. Dog owners should respect any regulations and not presume that strangers are eager to meet their pet. Keep your pet under physical control whenever other people are approaching.

Best Hikes in Massachusetts

Can't decide where to hike this weekend? Here are my picks for the best hikes in several categories:

Top Trails for Fall Foliage Viewing

Mount Greylock: Rounds Rock, Berkshires and Western Massachusetts, page 44. This easy one-mile loop to a pair of ledges offers some of the most dramatic views on Mount Greylock—for little effort.

Monument Mountain, Berkshires and Western Massachusetts, page 64. An easy trek, with blooming mountain laurel in the summer and glorious foliage in autumn.

Mount Everett, Berkshires and Western Massachusetts, page 76. From this 2,602-foot summit, you'll get long views of the rolling, forested hills of southwestern Massachusetts, not to mention that you'll pass several waterfalls along the way.

Mount Watatic and Nutting Hill, Central Massachusetts, page 98. This little hill offers big views extending as far as Mount Monadnock in New Hampshire and Wachusett Mountain.

Noanet Woodlands, Greater Boston and Cape Cod, page 161. Stroll through quiet forest to a view across wooded hills of the Boston skyline 20 miles away.

foliage view on Monument Mountain

COURTESY OF THE BERKSHIRE VISITORS BUREAU

Top Coastline Hikes

Bar Head Drumlin/Plum Island, Greater Boston and Cape Cod, page 140. Combining sandy beach, rocky shores, and terrain shaped by a receding glacier some 10,000 years ago, this easy hike offers far more than your usual coastal stroll.

Province Lands Trail, Greater Boston and Cape Cod, page 179. Possibly the most interesting paved path on the planet, this winds amid sand dunes, forest, and ponds.

Great Island Trail, Greater Boston and Cape Cod, page 181. Classic Cape Cod, this six-mile trail features sandy dunes and expansive bay views.

Atlantic White Cedar Swamp, Greater Boston and Cape Cod, page 183. Stroll a mile-long boardwalk through a dark forest, stunted oak and pine, taller pitch pine, black and white oak, golden beach-heather, and broom crowberry—many twisted by almost constant winds.

Aquinnah, Greater Boston and Cape Cod, page 190. This easy beach stroll out at the western point of Martha's Vineyard leads to colorful cliffs perfect for sunset watching.

Top Hikes to Waterfalls

Mount Greylock: Money Brook Falls, Berkshires and Western Massachusetts, page 30. The biggest waterfall on the biggest hill in the Bay State is hidden away in quiet woods.

Mount Greylock: March Cataract Falls, Berkshires and Western Massachusetts, page 40. An easy, one-mile walk brings you to this 30-foot waterfall. (See both these falls and Money Brook Falls on the Mount Greylock Circuit, page 33.)

Mount Everett, Berkshires and Western Massachusetts, page 76. Pass several waterfalls on the trail to the summit of this 2,602-foot peak.

Bash Bish Falls, Berkshires and Western Massachusetts, page 82. Though worth a trip year-round, spring snowmelt enhances this dramatic, boulder-strewn cascade.

Hubbard River Gorge, Berkshires and Western Massachusetts, page 86. The Hubbard River drops 450 feet over 2.5 miles through numerous waterfalls and cascades.

Top Hikes Longer Than 5 Miles

Mount Greylock Circuit, Berkshires and Western Massachusetts, page 32. This 12-mile loop takes in the mountain's highlights, from waterfalls to quiet forest to ridgeline hiking on the Appalachian Trail.

The Riga Plateau, Berkshires and Western Massachusetts, page 79. A lovely, 17-mile stretch of the Appalachian Trail with easy, ridge-top terrain and long views.

Alander Mountain, Berkshires and Western Massachusetts, page 84. Although it's 5.6 miles round-trip, this easy hike only ascends about 500 vertical feet, so the long views as far as New York's Catskill Mountains aren't paid for with a lot of sweat and soreness.

Hubbard River Gorge, Berkshires and Western Massachusetts, page 86. This six-mile loop drops through the gorge and circles back through quiet woods.

Middlesex Fells Skyline Trail, Greater Boston and Cape Cod, page 157. This seven-mile loop is the premier hiking circuit in the Fells, a 2,000-acre piece of woods in an urban wilderness. It traverses countless rocky ledges, some with good views of the Fells and the Boston skyline.

looking out from the top of Mount Greylock

Top Easy and Scenic Walks

Mount Greylock: Rounds Rock, Berkshires and Western Massachusetts, page 44. Good for small kids, this short trail leads to several lookout points facing Mount Greylock.

Mount Watatic and Nutting Hill, Central Massachusetts, page 98. Less than three miles long, this loop over Mount Watatic's 1,832-foot, bald crown offers views on a clear day of Wachusett Mountain, Mount Monadnock, the entire Wapack Range, the White Mountains, and the Boston skyline.

Maudslay State Park, Greater Boston and Cape Cod, page 138. Visitors here can take in the park's lovely gardens and mountain laurels, or sit in on park-sponsored educational events.

World's End, Greater Boston and Cape Cod, page 172. A bevy of interconnecting carriage paths, designed in the late 1800s by famed landscape architect Frederick Law Olmsted, today provides views of Boston's skyline.

Nauset Marsh, Greater Boston and Cape Cod, page 186. Just over a mile long, this loop trail is well marked and features interpretive signs about the marsh and its varied plant life.

Top Hikes for Children

Pine Cobble, Berkshires and Western Massachusetts, page 28. Short, fairly easy, and the "top" feels like a summit, with its sweeping view of the Hoosic Valley and Mount Greylock—a perfect outing for kids.

Crow Hills, Central Massachusetts, page 102. This gentle loop crams a lot into 0.7 miles—the varied scenery includes cliffs, forests, and ponds.

Purgatory Chasm, Central Massachusetts, page 124. This short loop has not a moment of boredom, and kids will love scrambling around the boulders and rock formations.

Great Meadows National Wildlife Refuge, Greater Boston and Cape Cod, page 150. An easy, two-mile stroll through prime birding territory—kids will love spotting herons, wood ducks, and other marshland inhabitants.

Great Island Trail, Greater Boston and Cape Cod, page 181. This lonely beach presents endless adventure for young minds, from scurrying crabs to sand dunes to explore.

Top Hikes for Bird-Watching

Wachusett Meadow to Wachusett Mountain, Central Massachusetts, page 119. Expansive views with long sight lines provide ample opportunity to spot birds in flight.

Bar Head Drumlin/Plum Island, Greater Boston and Cape Cod, page 140. This place is on the must-see list for all serious birders.

Great Meadows National Wildlife Refuge, Greater Boston and Cape Cod, page 150. One of the best birding regions in Massachusetts; over 200 species of birds have been spotted in this 3,000-acre refuge.

World's End, Greater Boston and Cape Cod, page 172. Come in spring and fall to see a variety of migratory birds.

Caratunk Wildlife Refuge, Greater Boston and Cape Cod, page 174. A favorite for migratory birds, this wildlife refuge features a loop trail through wetlands.

Top Hikes to Watch the Sunrise

Pine Cobble, Berkshires and Western Massachusetts, page 28. A short, accessible pre-dawn hike gets you to this sweeping view of the Hoosic Valley and Mount Greylock.

Crow Hills, Central Massachusetts, page 102. Reaching the ledges atop these cliffs won't take you too long, and the view of sunlight slanting over the wooded hills and ponds of Leominster State Forest is one of the best in central Massachusetts.

Bar Head Drumlin/Plum Island, Greater Boston and Cape Cod, page 140. Begin your day with cormorants, herons, and kingfishers at the nearby Parker River National Wildlife Refuge.

Halibut Point, Greater Boston and Cape Cod, page 146. Ease into your day with a relaxing amble around this rocky shore.

Middlesex Fells Skyline Trail, Greater Boston and Cape Cod, page 157. From the top of Pine Hill, near the start of this loop, watch the sunrise over Boston's skyline and the Blue Hills to the south.

Top Hikes to Watch the Sunset

Mount Tom, Berkshires and Western Massachusetts, page 72. Imposing basalt cliffs and wide open views of the Berkshires are part of this popular hike's appeal.

Alander Mountain, Berkshires and Western Massachusetts, page

84. Long views west as far as New York's Catskill Mountains make this a premier spot to watch the sun drop over the distant horizon.

Mount Holyoke, Central Massachusetts, page 122. Pause at one of the open views westward along this up-and-down ridgeline to see the sun drop over the Connecticut Valley and distant Berkshires.

Great Island Trail, Greater Boston and Cape Cod, page 181. A favorite for watching the sun set into Cape Cod Bay.

Aquinnah, Greater Boston and Cape Cod, page 190. Bring a picnic and watch the sunset on this easy beach walk.

© MICHAEL LANZA

The Berkshires and Western Massachusetts

The Berkshires and Western Massachusetts

The rural hills west of the Connecticut River harbor the best opportunities in Massachusetts for longer day hikes and backpacking trips. The Bay State's highest peak, 3,491-foot Mount Greylock, and other summits in the Berkshires offer scenic, sometimes rugged trails with occasional far-reaching views of these green, rounded hills.

The Appalachian Trail runs for 90 miles through the Berkshires, with such highlights as Mount Greylock and the beautiful Riga Plateau; both are popular destinations for day hiking and backpacking, especially from July through September, when camping areas tend to fill up quickly on weekends. But both are also far enough south and low enough that the prime hiking season often begins by mid-spring and lasts through late autumn. I backpacked the Riga Plateau one May and found the trees in full, leafy bloom, the temperature comfortably warm, the bugs barely noticeable, and few other people on the trail. Winters are typically cold and see plenty of snow in the hills, and several of these hikes make excellent, easy-to-moderate outings on snowshoes or cross-country skis.

The Appalachian Trail does tend to draw the heaviest hiker traffic, though, and there's plenty of other fine hiking in western Massachusetts, from state forests with hidden gems like Alander Mountain and the Hubbard River Gorge to private reserves like Monument Mountain, and one of New England's most beautiful waterfalls, Bash Bish Falls.

Along the Appalachian Trail, dogs must be kept under control, and bikes, horses, hunting, and firearms are prohibited. In state parks and forests, dogs must be leashed; horses are allowed in most state forests and parks, as is hunting in season.

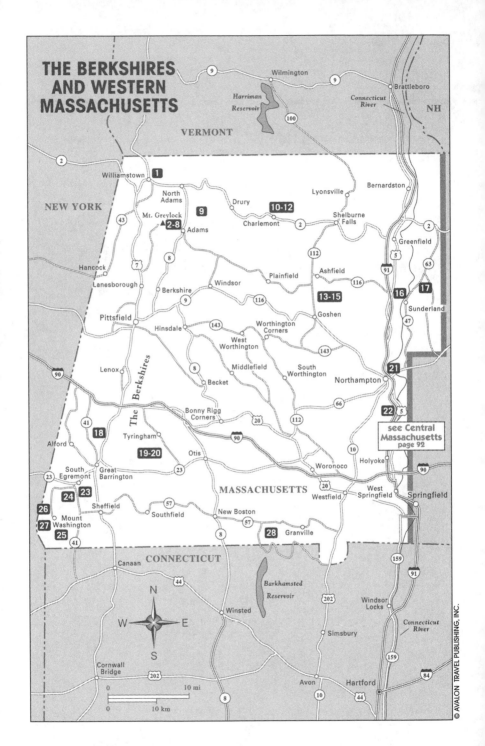

THE BERKSHIRES
AND WESTERN
MASSACHUSETTS

VERMONT

NEW YORK

Harriman Reservoir

Wilmington

Connecticut River

Brattleboro

NH

Williamstown

North Adams

Mt. Greylock

Adams

Drury

Charlemont

Lyonsville

Shelburne Falls

Bernardston

Greenfield

Sunderland

Hancock

Lanesborough

Berkshire

Windsor

Plainfield

Ashfield

Pittsfield

Hinsdale

West Worthington

Worthington Corners

Goshen

Northampton

Lenox

The Berkshires

Becket

Middlefield

South Worthington

Alford

Tyringham

Bonny Rigg Corners

Otis

Woronoco

Holyoke

South Egremont

Great Barrington

Sheffield

Southfield

New Boston

Granville

Westfield

West Springfield

Springfield

MASSACHUSETTS

Mount Washington

see Central Massachusetts page 92

Canaan

CONNECTICUT

Barkhamsted Reservoir

Winsted

Windsor Locks

N
W   E
S

Simsbury

Connecticut River

Cornwall Bridge

Avon

Hartford

0   10 mi

0   10 km

© AVALON TRAVEL PUBLISHING, INC.

Contents

1 PINE COBBLE

in Williamstown

Total distance: 3.2 miles round-trip   **Hiking time:** 2 hours

Difficulty: 3   **Rating:** 8

I began backpacking Vermont's Long Trail from this access trail rather than using the Appalachian Trail (which crosses MA 2 in the North Adams Blackinton section) because the view from Pine Cobble makes for a much more auspicious start to a long hike. Here in Massachusetts's northwest corner, the extensive quartzite ledges on the top of 1,894-foot Pine Cobble offer excellent views of the Hoosic Valley, the low, green hills flanking the river, and towering Mount Greylock. Ascending at an easy to moderate grade, this 3.2-mile trek is popular with students at nearby Williams College and is a good outing for young children. It climbs about 900 feet in elevation.

From the parking area, walk across Pine Cobble Road to the trail. Follow the trail's blue blazes and well-worn path. In less than a mile, a side path on the right leads 350 feet downhill to Bear Spring. At 1.5 miles from the parking area, the blue blazes hook sharply left and a spur path leads to the right 0.1 mile to Pine Cobble's summit. Take the spur path, soon reaching a ledge that offers a view west to the Taconic Range. About 100 feet farther uphill is the summit. The best views are from the open ledges about 30 feet beyond the summit. Looking south (right) you see Mount Greylock; east lie the Clarksburg State Forest's woods and hills, and to the north extends an array of hills traversed by Appalachian Trail hikers on their way into Vermont. Return the same way you came.

Special note: Hikers interested in a longer outing can continue north on the Pine Cobble Trail 0.5 mile to the Appalachian Trail, turn left (north), and hike another 0.5 mile to a view south of Mount Greylock from Eph's Lookout. The added distance makes the entire round-trip 5.2 miles.

User Groups

Hikers, snowshoers, and dogs. No wheelchair facilities. This trail is not suitable for bikes, horses, or skis. Hunting is prohibited.

Access and Fees
Parking and access are free.

Maps
For a map of hiking trails, refer to map 1 in the *Map and Guide to the Appalachian Trail in Massachusetts and Connecticut,* a five-map set and guidebook available for $19.95 ($14.95 for the maps alone) from the Appalachian Trail Conference. For a topographic area map, request North Adams from USGS Map Sales, Federal Center, Box 25286, Denver, CO 80225, 888/ASK-USGS (888/275-8747), website: http://mapping.usgs.gov.

Directions
From the junction of U.S. 7 and MA 2 in Williamstown, drive east on MA 2 for 0.6 mile, then turn left on Cole Avenue at the first traffic light. Drive another 0.8 mile, crossing a bridge over the Hoosic River and crossing railroad tracks, then turn right on North Housac Road. Follow it 0.4 mile to a left turn onto Pine Cobble Road and continue to the parking area 0.2 mile up on the left, across the street from the trailhead.

Contact
Appalachian Trail Conference, 799 Washington Street, P.O. Box 807, Harpers Ferry, WV 25425-0807, 304/535-6331, website: www.appalachiantrail.org.

2 MOUNT GREYLOCK: MONEY BROOK FALLS

in Mount Greylock State Reservation in Williamstown, North Adams, Adams, and Lanesborough

Total distance: 5 miles round-trip   **Hiking time:** 3 hours

Difficulty: 5   **Rating:** 9

Money Brook Falls tumbles from an impressive height into a ravine choked with trees that haven't survived the steep, erosive terrain. Despite being one of the most spectacular natural features on the biggest hill in the Bay State, it may be Massachusetts's best-kept secret. The trail makes several stream crossings, some of which could be difficult in high water.

From the parking area, walk past the gate onto the Hopper Trail and follow a flat, grassy lane 0.2 mile. Where the Hopper Trail diverges right, continue straight ahead on the Money Brook Trail. It ascends gently at first, but after passing the Mount Prospect Trail junction at 1.5 miles, it goes through some short, steep stretches. At 2.4 miles, turn right onto a side path that leads 0.1 mile to the falls. Hike back the way you came.

User Groups

Hikers, snowshoers, and dogs. Dogs must be leashed. No wheelchair facilities. This trail is not suitable for horses or skis. Bikes are prohibited. Hunting is allowed in season.

Access and Fees

A daily fee of $2 is collected from mid-May to mid-October at some parking areas. From the mid-December close of hunting season through mid-May, roads within the state reservation are closed to vehicles (and groomed for snowmobiles), but Hopper Road is maintained to this trailhead. There is a lean-to and a dispersed backcountry camping zone along the Money Brook Trail.

Maps

A free trail map of Mount Greylock State Reservation is available at the visitors center or at the Massachusetts Division of State

Parks and Recreation website. The *Northern Berkshires/Southwestern Massachusetts/Wachusett Mountain* map costs $5.95 in paper from the Appalachian Mountain Club, 800/262-4455, website: www .outdoors.org. The *Mount Greylock Reservation Trail Map* is $3.95 from New England Cartographics, 413/549-4124 or toll-free 888/995-6277, website: www.necartographics.com. These trails are also covered on map 1 in the *Map and Guide to the Appalachian Trail in Massachusetts and Connecticut,* a five-map set available for $19.95 ($14.95 for the maps alone) from the Appalachian Trail Conference. For topographic area maps, request North Adams and Cheshire from USGS Map Sales, Federal Center, Box 25286, Denver, CO 80225, 888/ASK-USGS (888/275-8747), website: http://mapping.usgs.gov.

Directions
From Route 43, 2.5 miles south of the junction of Routes 43 and 2 in Williamstown and 2.3 miles north of the junction of Route 43 and U.S. 7, turn east onto Hopper Road at a sign for Mount Hope Park. Drive 1.4 miles and bear left onto a dirt road. Continue 0.7 mile to the parking area on the right.

Contact
Mount Greylock State Reservation, P.O. Box 138, Rockwell Road, Lanesborough, MA 01237, 413/499-4262 or 413/499-4263. Massachusetts Division of State Parks and Recreation, 251 Causeway Street, Suite 600, Boston, MA 02114-2104, 617/626-1250, website: www.state.ma.us/dem/forparks.htm. Appalachian Trail Conference, P.O. Box 807, Harpers Ferry, WV 25425, 304/535-6331, website: www.appalachiantrail.org.

3 MOUNT GREYLOCK CIRCUIT

in Mount Greylock State Reservation in Williamstown,
North Adams, Adams, and Lanesborough

Total distance: 12 miles round-trip   **Hiking time:** 8 hours

Difficulty: 8   **Rating:** 10

Wanting to hike a loop around Massachusetts's highest peak,
3,491-foot Mount Greylock, taking in as many of its best features
as possible on a day hike, I devised this 12-mile circuit. It climbs
through and loops around the spectacular glacial cirque known
as the Hopper, passes two waterfalls, travels over the summit, follows a stretch of the Appalachian Trail, and then descends
through the rugged ravine of beautiful Money Brook. You could
shave this distance by two miles by skipping the side trail to
March Cataract Falls, and another mile by skipping Robinson
Point. This entire hike gains more than 2,500 feet in elevation.

From the parking area, walk past the gate onto the Hopper
Trail and follow a flat, grassy lane 0.2 mile to where the Money
Brook Trail leads straight ahead. Bear right with the Hopper
Trail, ascending an old logging road, somewhat steeply at times,
another two miles until you reach Sperry Road. Turn left and

near the summit of Mount Greylock

walk the road 0.1 mile; just before the parking area on the right, turn left on a dirt campground road. Walk about 200 feet, past the Chimney Group Camping Area, and turn left at a sign for the March Cataract Falls Trail. It leads a mile, descending through switchbacks, to March Cataract Falls, a 30-foot falls that usually maintains a flow even during dry seasons.

Backtrack to Sperry Road, turn left, walk about 100 yards past the parking area, and then turn left at a sign onto the Hopper Trail. The wide path climbs at a moderate grade past a short falls. Where the Deer Hill Trail diverges right, bear left. Within a mile of Sperry Road, where the Hopper Trail makes a sharp right, turn left onto the Overlook Trail. You reach the first view of the Hopper within minutes, though trees partially obstruct it. A half mile down the Overlook Trail lies the second view, which is better; Stony Ledge is visible across the Hopper to the west. Continue on the Overlook Trail to the paved Notch Road, 1.2 miles from the Hopper Trail junction. Turn left and walk the road downhill 0.1 mile, past a day-use parking turnout, then turn left onto a trail marked by blue blazes. It descends steeply 0.2 mile to Robinson Point and a view of the Hopper superior to anything on the Overlook Trail. Double back to the Overlook Trail, cross Notch Road, and follow the Overlook uphill for 0.4 mile to the white-blazed Appalachian Trail. Turn left on the Appalachian Trail, following it across the parking lot to the summit, where you find the War Memorial Tower and the Bascom Lodge. The best views are to the east from the meadow beyond the tower; there are also good views to the west.

From the tower, follow the Appalachian Trail north. About a mile from the summit is a good eastern view. About 2.4 miles from the summit, a side trail leads left to Notch Road, but continue 0.2 mile straight ahead on the Appalachian Trail over Mount Williams, one of Greylock's summits. The Appalachian Trail swings left here, descending easily 0.9 mile to Notch Road. Cross the road and, 0.1 mile into the woods, turn left onto the Money Brook Trail; in 0.2 mile, pass a short side path leading to the Wilbur's Clearing shelter. The trail reaches a side path 0.7 mile beyond the shelter that leads a short distance to spectacular Money Brook Falls. Backtrack from the falls on the side path and continue on the Money Brook Trail, following the brook through a wild, narrow valley, with a few crossings that could be tricky in high water. Nearly a mile past the falls, the Mount Prospect Trail branches right; stay on the Money Brook Trail another 1.5 miles to the Hopper Trail—passing a dispersed camping zone just before reaching the Hopper Trail—then continue straight ahead 0.2 mile to return to the parking area.

User Groups
Hikers and dogs. Dogs must be leashed. No wheelchair facilities. This trail should not be attempted in winter except by hikers prepared for severe winter weather, and is not suitable for horses or skis. Bikes are prohibited. Hunting is allowed in season.

Access and Fees
A daily fee of $2 is collected from mid-May to mid-October at some parking areas. From the mid-December close of hunting season through mid-May, roads within the state reservation are closed to vehicles (and groomed for snowmobiles), but Hopper Road is maintained to this trailhead. There is a lean-to and a dispersed backcountry camping zone along the Money Brook Trail. Contact the Mount Greylock State Reservation about whether the Bascom Lodge on the mountain's summit is open; it was formerly managed by the Appalachian Mountain Club.

Maps
A free, basic trail map of Mount Greylock State Reservation is available at the visitors center or at the Massachusetts Division of State Parks and Recreation website. The *Northern Berkshires/Southwestern Massachusetts/Wachusett Mountain* map costs $5.95 in paper from the Appalachian Mountain Club, 800/262-4455, website: www.outdoors.org. The *Mount Greylock Reservation Trail Map* is $3.95 from New England Cartographics, 413/549-4124 or toll-free 888/995-6277, website: www.necartographics.com. These trails are also covered on map 1 in the *Map and Guide to the Appalachian Trail in Massachusetts and Connecticut,* a five-map set available for $19.95 ($14.95 for the maps alone) from the Appalachian Trail Conference. For topographic area maps, request North Adams and Cheshire from USGS Map Sales, Federal Center, Box 25286,

Denver, CO 80225, 888/ASK-USGS (888/275-8747), website: http://mapping.usgs.gov.

Directions

From Route 43, 2.5 miles south of the junction of Routes 43 and 2 in Williamstown and 2.3 miles north of the junction of Route 43 and U.S. 7, turn east onto Hopper Road at a sign for Mount Hope Park. Drive 1.4 miles and bear left onto a dirt road. Continue 0.7 mile to the parking area on the right.

Contact

Mount Greylock State Reservation, P.O. Box 138, Rockwell Road, Lanesborough, MA 01237, 413/499-4262 or 413/499-4263. Massachusetts Division of State Parks and Recreation, 251 Causeway Street, Suite 600, Boston, MA 02114-2104, 617/626-1250, website: www.state.ma.us/dem/forparks.htm. Appalachian Trail Conference, P.O. Box 807, Harpers Ferry, WV 25425, 304/535-6331, website: www.appalachiantrail.org.

4 MOUNT GREYLOCK: ROBINSON POINT

in Mount Greylock State Reservation in Williamstown, North
Adams, Adams, and Lanesborough

Total distance: 0.4 miles round-trip   **Hiking time:** 0.5 hour

Difficulty: 2   **Rating:** 8

The high ledge at Robinson Point offers one of the best views on
Greylock of the Hopper, the huge glacial cirque carved out of the
mountain's northwest flank. Visible are Stony Ledge, at the end
of the ridge forming the Hopper's western wall; Williamstown, in
the valley beyond the Hopper's mouth; and the Taconic Range on
the horizon. From the turnout, walk downhill just a few steps and
then turn left onto a trail marked by blue blazes. It descends
steeply 0.2 mile to Robinson Point. Return the same way.

User Groups

Hikers and dogs. Dogs must be leashed. No wheelchair facilities.
This trail is not suitable for horses or skis. The trailhead is not
accessible by road in winter for snowshoeing. Bikes are prohibited. Hunting is allowed in season.

Access and Fees

A daily fee of $2 is collected from mid-May to mid-October at
some parking areas. From the mid-December close of hunting
season through mid-May, roads within the state reservation are
closed to vehicles (and groomed for snowmobiles). This trailhead
is not accessible by car in the winter months.

Maps

A free, basic trail map of Mount Greylock State Reservation is
available at the visitors center or at the Massachusetts Division of
State Parks and Recreation website. The *Northern Berkshires/South-
western Massachusetts/Wachusett Mountain* map costs $5.95 in paper
from the Appalachian Mountain Club, 800/262-4455, website:
www.outdoors.org. The *Mount Greylock Reservation Trail Map* is
$3.95 from New England Cartographics, 413/549-4124 or toll-free
888/995-6277, website: www.necartographics.com. These trails are
also covered on map 1 in the *Map and Guide to the Appalachian Trail*

in Massachusetts and Connecticut, a five-map set available for $19.95 ($14.95 for the maps alone) from the Appalachian Trail Conference. For topographic area maps, request North Adams and Cheshire from USGS Map Sales, Federal Center, Box 25286, Denver, CO 80225, 888/ASK-USGS (888/275-8747), website: http://mapping.usgs.gov.

Directions

From MA 2, 3.7 miles east of the junction of Routes 2 and 43 in Williamstown and 1.3 miles west of the junction of Routes 2 and 8A in North Adams, turn south onto Notch Road. Follow Notch Road up the mountain for 7.4 miles to a turnout for day-use parking on the right. From U.S. 7 in Lanesborough, 1.3 miles north of town center and 4.2 miles south of the Lanesborough/ New Ashford line, turn east onto North Main Street. Drive 0.7 mile and turn right onto Quarry Road. Continue 0.6 mile and bear left at a sign reading "Rockwell Road to Greylock." The Greylock Visitor Center is 0.6 mile farther up that road. From the visitors center, follow Rockwell Road up the mountain for 7.2 miles, turn left onto Notch Road, and continue 0.9 mile to the day-use parking turnout on the left.

Contact

Mount Greylock State Reservation, P.O. Box 138, Rockwell Road, Lanesborough, MA 01237, 413/499-4262 or 413/499-4263. Massachusetts Division of State Parks and Recreation, 251 Causeway Street, Suite 600, Boston, MA 02114-2104, 617/626-1250, website: www.state.ma.us/dem/forparks.htm. Appalachian Trail Conference, P.O. Box 807, Harpers Ferry, WV 25425, 304/535-6331, website: www.appalachiantrail.org.

5 MOUNT GREYLOCK: DEER HILL TRAIL

in Mount Greylock State Reservation in Williamstown, North
Adams, Adams, and Lanesborough

Total distance: 2.2 miles round-trip   **Hiking time:** 1.5 hours

Difficulty: 2   **Rating:** 8

A friend and I actually backpacked this fairly easy two-mile loop
past Deer Hill Falls and an interesting grove of tall hemlocks one
weekend, and spent the night at the lean-to along the way, listen-
ing to coyotes in the darkness. If you have time, walk or drive
the mile to the end of Sperry Road for the view from Stony
Ledge of the huge glacial cirque on Greylock known as the Hopper. It is perhaps the finest view on the mountain.

From the parking area, walk back up Sperry Road (south) for
0.4 mile and turn right onto the Deer Hill Trail. The flat, wide
path crosses a brook and within 0.4 mile makes a right turn, descending past a dark grove of tall hemlocks on the left and reaching the lean-to one mile from the road. Just beyond the lean-to,
the trail descends abruptly, crosses over a stream on a wooden
bridge, and then climbs steeply up to Deer Hill Falls. About 0.2
mile above the falls, make a right turn onto the Roaring Brook
Trail, which leads back to the parking area in 0.1 mile.

User Groups

Hikers, snowshoers, and dogs. Dogs must be leashed. No wheelchair facilities. This trail is not suitable for horses or skis. Bikes
are prohibited. Hunting is allowed in season.

Access and Fees

A daily fee of $2 is collected from mid-May to mid-October at
some parking areas. From the mid-December close of hunting
season through mid-May, roads within the state reservation are
closed to vehicles (and groomed for snowmobiles). This trailhead
is not accessible by car in winter. There is a lean-to for overnight
camping along the Deer Hill Trail.

Maps

A free, basic trail map of Mount Greylock State Reservation is available at the visitors center or at the Massachusetts Division of State Parks and Recreation website. The *Northern Berkshires/Southwestern Massachusetts/Wachusett Mountain* map costs $5.95 in paper from the Appalachian Mountain Club, 800/262-4455, website: www.outdoors.org. The *Mount Greylock Reservation Trail Map* is $3.95 from New England Cartographics, 413/549-4124 or toll-free 888/995-6277, website: www.necartographics.com. These trails are also covered on map 1 in the *Map and Guide to the Appalachian Trail in Massachusetts and Connecticut,* a five-map set available for $19.95 ($14.95 for the maps alone) from the Appalachian Trail Conference. For topographic area maps, request North Adams and Cheshire from USGS Map Sales, Federal Center, Box 25286, Denver, CO 80225, 888/ASK-USGS (888/275-8747), website: http://mapping.usgs.gov.

Directions
From MA 2, 3.7 miles east of the junction of Routes 2 and 43 in Williamstown and 1.3 miles west of the junction of Routes 2 and 8A in North Adams, turn south onto Notch Road. Follow Notch Road up the mountain for 8.3 miles and turn right onto Rockwell Road. Continue 1.7 miles, turn right onto Sperry Road, and drive 0.6 mile to the roadside parking. From U.S. 7 in Lanesborough, 1.3 miles north of the town center and 4.2 miles south of the Lanesborough/New Ashford line, turn east onto North Main Street. Drive 0.7 mile and turn right onto Quarry Road. Continue 0.6 mile and bear left at a sign reading "Rockwell Road to Greylock." The Greylock Visitor Center is 0.6 mile farther up that road. From the visitors center, follow Rockwell Road up the mountain for 5.5 miles, turn left onto Sperry Road, and continue 0.6 mile to the parking area.

Contact
Mount Greylock State Reservation, P.O. Box 138, Rockwell Road, Lanesborough, MA 01237, 413/499-4262 or 413/499-4263. Massachusetts Division of State Parks and Recreation, 251 Causeway Street, Suite 600, Boston, MA 02114-2104, 617/626-1250, website: www.state.ma.us/dem/forparks.htm. Appalachian Trail Conference, P.O. Box 807, Harpers Ferry, WV 25425, 304/535-6331, website: www.appalachiantrail.org.

6 MOUNT GREYLOCK: MARCH CATARACT FALLS

in Mount Greylock State Reservation in Williamstown, North
Adams, Adams, and Lanesborough

Total distance: 2 miles round-trip   **Hiking time:** 1.5 hours

Difficulty: 2   **Rating:** 8

March Cataract Falls is a 30-foot-high water curtain at the end of
a fairly easy one-mile trail beginning in the Sperry Road Campground. From the parking area, cross the road onto a dirt campground road. Walk that short half-circle road to the March
Cataract Falls Trail, marked by a sign. It starts out on easy
ground and then descends through switchbacks, reaching March
Cataract Falls a mile from the campground. Head back along
the same route.

User Groups
Hikers and dogs. Dogs must be leashed. No wheelchair facilities.
This trail is not suitable for horses or skis. The trailhead is not
accessible by road in winter for snowshoeing. Bikes are prohibited. Hunting is allowed in season.

Access and Fees
A daily fee of $2 is collected from mid-May to mid-October at
some parking areas. From the mid-December close of hunting
season through mid-May, roads in the state reservation are
closed to vehicles (and groomed for snowmobiles). This trailhead
is not accessible by car in winter.

Maps
A free, basic trail map of Mount Greylock State Reservation is
available at the visitors center or at the Massachusetts Division
of State Parks and Recreation website. The *Northern Berkshires/
Southwestern Massachusetts/Wachusett Mountain* map costs $5.95 in
paper from the Appalachian Mountain Club, 800/262-4455, website: www.outdoors.org. The *Mount Greylock Reservation Trail Map* is
$3.95 from New England Cartographics, 413/549-4124 or toll-free
888/995-6277, website: www.necartographics.com. These trails are

also covered on map 1 in the *Map and Guide to the Appalachian Trail in Massachusetts and Connecticut,* a five-map set available for $19.95 ($14.95 for the maps alone) from the Appalachian Trail Conference. For topographic area maps, request North Adams and Cheshire from USGS Map Sales, Federal Center, Box 25286, Denver, CO 80225, 888/ASK-USGS (888/275-8747), website: http://mapping.usgs.gov.

Directions

From MA 2, 3.7 miles east of the junction of Routes 2 and 43 in Williamstown and 1.3 miles west of the junction of Routes 2 and 8A in North Adams, turn south onto Notch Road. Follow Notch Road up the mountain for 8.3 miles and turn right onto Rockwell Road. Continue 1.7 miles, turn right onto Sperry Road, and drive 0.6 mile to the roadside parking. From U.S. 7 in Lanesborough, 1.3 miles north of the town center and 4.2 miles south of the Lanesborough/New Ashford line, turn east onto North Main Street. Drive 0.7 mile and turn right onto Quarry Road. Continue 0.6 mile and bear left at a sign reading "Rockwell Road to Greylock." The Greylock Visitor Center is 0.6 mile farther up that road. From the visitors center, follow Rockwell Road up the mountain for 5.5 miles, turn left onto Sperry Road, and continue 0.6 mile to the parking area.

Contact

Mount Greylock State Reservation, P.O. Box 138, Rockwell Road, Lanesborough, MA 01237, 413/499-4262 or 413/499-4263. Massachusetts Division of State Parks and Recreation, 251 Causeway Street, Suite 600, Boston, MA 02114-2104, 617/626-1250, website: www.state.ma.us/dem/forparks.htm. Appalachian Trail Conference, P.O. Box 807, Harpers Ferry, WV 25425, 304/535-6331, website: www.appalachiantrail.org.

7 MOUNT GREYLOCK: JONES NOSE

in Mount Greylock State Reservation in Williamstown, North
Adams, Adams, and Lanesborough

Total distance: 1 mile round-trip   **Hiking time:** 0.75 hour

Difficulty: 2   **Rating:** 8

Jones Nose is an open ledge on Greylock's southern ridge that
offers a broad view of the mountains to the south and west—a
nice spot to catch a sunset. From the parking area, walk north
on the Jones Nose Trail. It passes through woods, crosses a
meadow, and then ascends steeply to a side path on the left, 0.5
mile from the parking lot. Follow that path 40 feet to the view-
point. Return the way you came.

User Groups

Hikers and dogs. Dogs must be leashed. No wheelchair facilities.
This trail is not suitable for horses or skis. The trailhead is not
accessible by road in winter for snowshoeing. Bikes are prohibited. Hunting is allowed in season.

Access and Fees

A daily fee of $2 is collected from mid-May to mid-October at
some parking areas. From the mid-December close of hunting
season through mid-May, roads in the state reservation are
closed to vehicles (and groomed for snowmobiles). This trailhead
is not accessible by car in winter.

Maps

A free, basic trail map of Mount Greylock State Reservation is
available at the visitors center or at the Massachusetts Division of
State Parks and Recreation website. The *Northern Berkshires/South-
western Massachusetts/Wachusett Mountain* map costs $5.95 in paper
from the Appalachian Mountain Club, 800/262-4455, website:
www.outdoors.org. The *Mount Greylock Reservation Trail Map* is
$3.95 from New England Cartographics, 413/549-4124 or toll-free
888/995-6277, website: www.necartographics.com. These trails are
also covered on map 1 in the *Map and Guide to the Appalachian Trail
in Massachusetts and Connecticut,* a five-map set available for $19.95

($14.95 for the maps alone) from the Appalachian Trail Conference. For topographic area maps, request North Adams and Cheshire from USGS Map Sales, Federal Center, Box 25286, Denver, CO 80225, 888/ASK-USGS (888/275-8747), website: http://mapping.usgs.gov.

Directions

From MA 2, 3.7 miles east of the junction of Routes 2 and 43 in Williamstown and 1.3 miles west of the junction of Routes 2 and 8A in North Adams, turn south onto Notch Road. Follow Notch Road up the mountain for 8.3 miles and turn right onto Rockwell Road. Continue 3.5 miles to the Jones Nose parking lot on the left. From U.S. 7 in Lanesborough, 1.3 miles north of the town center and 4.2 miles south of the Lanesborough/New Ashford line, turn east onto North Main Street. Drive 0.7 mile and turn right onto Quarry Road. Continue 0.6 mile and bear left at a sign reading "Rockwell Road to Greylock." The Greylock Visitor Center is 0.6 mile farther up that road. From the visitors center, follow Rockwell Road up the mountain for 3.7 miles to the Jones Nose parking lot on the right.

Contact

Mount Greylock State Reservation, P.O. Box 138, Rockwell Road, Lanesborough, MA 01237, 413/499-4262 or 413/499-4263. Massachusetts Division of State Parks and Recreation, 251 Causeway Street, Suite 600, Boston, MA 02114-2104, 617/626-1250, website: www.state.ma.us/dem/forparks.htm. Appalachian Trail Conference, P.O. Box 807, Harpers Ferry, WV 25425, 304/535-6331, website: www.appalachiantrail.org.

8 MOUNT GREYLOCK: ROUNDS ROCK

in Mount Greylock State Reservation in Williamstown, North
Adams, Adams, and Lanesborough

Total distance: 1 mile round-trip   **Hiking time:** 0.75 hour

Difficulty: 1   **Rating:** 9

This easy one-mile loop to a pair of ledges offers some of the
most dramatic views on Mount Greylock—for little effort. This is
a terrific hike with young children or for catching a sunset or the
fall foliage. From the turnout, cross the road to the Rounds Rock
Trail. Follow it through woods and across blueberry patches
about a half mile to where a side path (at a sign that reads
"Scenic Vista") leads left about 75 yards to a sweeping view
south from atop a low cliff. Backtrack and turn left on the main
trail, following it 0.1 mile to another, shorter side path and a
view south and west. Complete the loop on the Rounds Rock
Trail by following it out to Rockwell Road. Turn right and walk
the road about 150 yards back to the turnout.

User Groups
Hikers and dogs. Dogs must be leashed. No wheelchair facilities.
This trail is not suitable for horses or skis. The trailhead is not
accessible by road in winter for snowshoeing. Bikes are prohibited. Hunting is allowed in season.

Access and Fees
A daily fee of $2 is collected from mid-May to mid-October at
some parking areas. From the mid-December close of hunting
season through mid-May, roads in the state reservation are
closed to vehicles (and groomed for snowmobiles). This trailhead
is not accessible by car in winter.

Maps
A free, basic trail map of Mount Greylock State Reservation is
available at the visitors center or at the Massachusetts Division of
State Parks and Recreation website. The *Northern Berkshires/
Southwestern Massachusetts/Wachusett Mountain* map costs $5.95 in
paper from the Appalachian Mountain Club, 800/262-4455, web-

site: www.outdoors.org. The *Mount Greylock Reservation Trail Map* is $3.95 from New England Cartographics, 413/549-4124 or toll-free 888/995-6277, website: www.necartographics.com. These trails are also covered on map 1 in the *Map and Guide to the Appalachian Trail in Massachusetts and Connecticut,* a five-map set available for $19.95 ($14.95 for the maps alone) from the Appalachian Trail Conference. For topographic area maps, request North Adams and Cheshire from USGS Map Sales, Federal Center, Box 25286, Denver, CO 80225, 888/ASK-USGS (888/275-8747), website: http://mapping.usgs.gov.

Directions
From MA 2, 3.7 miles east of the junction of Routes 2 and 43 in Williamstown and 1.3 miles west of the junction of Routes 2 and 8A in North Adams, turn south onto Notch Road. Follow Notch Road up the mountain for 8.3 miles and turn right onto Rockwell Road. Continue 4.2 miles to a turnout on the left, across from the Rounds Rock Trail. From U.S. 7 in Lanesborough, 1.3 miles north of the town center and 4.2 miles south of the Lanesborough/New Ashford line, turn east onto North Main Street. Drive 0.7 mile and turn right onto Quarry Road. Continue 0.6 mile and bear left at a sign reading "Rockwell Road to Greylock." The Greylock Visitor Center is 0.6 mile farther up that road. From the visitors center, follow Rockwell Road up the mountain for three miles to a turnout on the right, across from the Rounds Rock Trail.

Contact
Mount Greylock State Reservation, P.O. Box 138, Rockwell Road, Lanesborough, MA 01237, 413/499-4262 or 413/499-4263. Massachusetts Division of State Parks and Recreation, 251 Causeway Street, Suite 600, Boston, MA 02114-2104, 617/626-1250, website: www.state.ma.us/dem/forparks.htm. Appalachian Trail Conference, P.O. Box 807, Harpers Ferry, WV 25425, 304/535-6331, website: www.appalachiantrail.org.

⑨ SPRUCE HILL

in Savoy Mountain State Forest in North Adams, Adams, Florida, and Savoy

Total distance: 3 miles round-trip   **Hiking time:** 1.5 hours

Difficulty: 3   **Rating:** 8

This easy, three-mile hike provides some of the most attractive views possible in the state for a relatively minor effort; only the last stretch turns somewhat steep, and only briefly at that. Spruce Hill's summit is at 2,566 feet. The total elevation gained is about 1,200 feet. I camped out just below the Spruce Hill summit one night in early December. After dark, I hiked up onto the hill under a sky full of stars, overlooking the lights of the Hoosic Valley. The Savoy Mountain State Forest has about 48 miles of trails and roads for hiking, snowshoeing, mountain biking, and cross-country skiing. It is the fourth-largest piece, but one of the least-known pieces, of Bay State public land.

Walk 100 feet up the forest road and turn right onto a trail signed for "Spruce Hill, Hawk Lookout." Within 150 yards, the trail crosses a power line easement. About a quarter mile farther, it crosses a second set of power lines; just beyond those lines, continue straight onto the Busby Trail (marked by a sign), going uphill and following blue blazes. In a quarter mile or so, the trail crosses an old stone wall. Then, within the span of about a quarter mile, you cross a small brook, pass an old stone foundation on your right, and then pass over a stone wall. On the other side of that wall, another trail branches left, but continue straight ahead, still following the blue blazes. About 0.1 mile farther, the trail forks; both forks go to the summit, but the right option is easier and more direct, reaching the bare top of Spruce Hill within 0.25 mile.

Though a few low trees grow in isolated groves on the hilltop, the hill's several open areas provide excellent views in all directions. To the west lies the Hoosic River Valley, where Route 8 runs through the towns of Adams and North Adams. Farther northwest you can see Williamstown. Across the valley rises the highest peak in Massachusetts, 3,491-foot Mount Greylock, with a prominent war memorial tower on its summit. The Appalachian

Trail follows the obvious northern ridge on Greylock—and you might consider how busy that trail can be while you are enjoying the top of Spruce Hill by yourself. Descend the way you came.

User Groups
Hikers and dogs. Dogs must be leashed. No wheelchair facilities. This trail is not suitable for horses or skis. Bikes are prohibited. Hunting is allowed in season.

Access and Fees
A daily parking fee of $5 is collected from mid-May to mid-October.

Maps
A free, basic trail map of Savoy Mountain State Forest is available at the state forest headquarters or at the Massachusetts Division of State Parks and Recreation website. For topographic area maps, request North Adams, Cheshire, and Ashfield from USGS Map Sales, Federal Center, Box 25286, Denver, CO 80225, 888/ASK-USGS (888/275-8747), website: http://mapping.usgs.gov.

Directions
From MA 2 in Florida, 6.9 miles west of the Florida/Savoy town line and 0.4 mile east of the Florida/North Adams line, turn south onto Central Shaft Road. Continue 2.9 miles, following signs for the Savoy Mountain State Forest, to the headquarters on the right (where maps are available). Less than 0.1 mile beyond the headquarters, park at a turnout on the right at the Old Florida Road, an unmaintained, wide forest road.

Contact
Savoy Mountain State Forest, 260 Central Shaft Road, Florida, MA 01247, 413/663-8469. Massachusetts Division of State Parks and Recreation, 251 Causeway Street, Suite 600, Boston, MA 02114-2104, 617/626-1250, website: www.state.ma.us/dem/forparks.htm.

10 MOHAWK TRAIL
in Mohawk Trail State Forest in Charlemont

Total distance: 5 miles round-trip   **Hiking time:** 3.5 hours

Difficulty: 7   **Rating:** 7

This mostly wooded ridge walk follows a historical route: the original Mohawk Trail, used for hundreds of years by the area's Native Americans. There is one good view along the ridge, from Todd Mountain ledge overlooking the Cold River Valley. This hike ascends about 700 feet. From the parking area, continue up the paved road, bearing left toward the camping area where the road forks, then bearing right at a sign for the Indian Trail at 0.7 mile. The trail remains flat for only about 200 feet, then turns right, and begins the steep and relentless ascent 0.5 mile to the ridge. This trail is not well marked and can be easy to lose in a few places. Once atop the ridge, the walking grows much easier. Turn right onto the Todd Mountain Trail, following it 0.5 mile to an open ledge with a good view. Double back to the Indian Trail and continue straight ahead on the Clark Mountain Trail; you will see disks on trees indicating that this is the old Mohawk Trail. This easy, wide path predates European settlement here by hundreds of years. About 0.8 mile past the Todd Mountain Trail, the Clark Mountain/Mohawk Trail swings right and begins descending; double back from here and descend the Indian Trail back to the start.

User Groups
Hikers and dogs. Dogs must be leashed. No wheelchair facilities. This trail would be difficult to snowshoe, and is not suitable for bikes, horses, or skis. Hunting is allowed in season.

Access and Fees
A daily parking fee of $5 is collected from mid-May to mid-October.

Maps
A free, basic trail and contour map of Mohawk Trail State Forest is available at the state forest headquarters or at the Massachusetts Division of State Parks and Recreation website. For a

topographic area map, request Rowe from USGS Map Sales, Federal Center, Box 25286, Denver, CO 80225, 888/ASK-USGS (888/275-8747), website: http://mapping.usgs.gov.

Directions

The main entrance to the Mohawk Trail State Forest is on MA 2, 3.7 miles west of the junction of Routes 2 and 8A in Charlemont and one mile east of the Savoy/Charlemont line. Drive the state forest road for 0.2 mile, through a gate, and park just beyond the gate on the left, behind the headquarters building.

Contact

Mohawk Trail State Forest, P.O. Box 7, MA 2, Charlemont, MA 01339, 413/339-5504. Massachusetts Division of State Parks and Recreation, 251 Causeway Street, Suite 600, Boston, MA 02114-2104, 617/626-1250, website: www.state.ma.us/dem/forparks.htm.

11 GIANT TREES OF CLARK RIDGE
in Mohawk Trail State Forest in Charlemont

Total distance: 1 mile round-trip   **Hiking time:** 2 hours

Difficulty: 2   **Rating:** 8

If you're wondering how it could take two hours to walk a mile, then consider this: You may not even walk a mile, yet you may spend even longer in here. Unlike the other hikes in this book, this one doesn't follow an established trail. It begins on an abandoned, somewhat overgrown logging road and becomes a bushwhack. But the steep, rugged terrain you encounter on the north flank of Clark Ridge is probably a big part of the reason loggers left so many giant trees untouched here over the past few centuries—a time period during which most of New England was deforested. Within an area of about 75 acres are an uncounted number of sugar maple, red oak, white ash, beech, and other hardwoods reaching more than 120 feet into the sky, and aged 200 to 300 years. One respected regional expert has identified a 160-foot white pine here as the tallest living thing in New England. It would be impossible for me to direct you to particular trees, and equally difficult for you to identify any individual tree by its height without the proper equipment. But, just as I did, I think you will find walking around in this cathedral of bark to be a rare and stirring experience.

From either parking area, walk across the bridge and immediately turn left, following a faint footpath down across a wash and a cleared area and onto a distinct trail—actually an abandoned logging road. The road dissipates within about a half mile, but you need only walk a quarter mile or so, then turn right, and bushwhack uphill. You soon find yourself craning your neck constantly. Be sure to remember how to find your way back to the logging road.

User Groups
Hikers, snowshoers, and dogs. Dogs must be leashed. No wheelchair facilities. This trail is not suitable for bikes, horses, or skis. Hunting is allowed in season.

Access and Fees

A daily parking fee of $5 is collected from mid-May to mid-October at some trailheads.

Maps

A free, basic trail and contour map of the Mohawk Trail State Forest is available at the state forest headquarters (reached via the state forest's main entrance) or at the Massachusetts Division of State Parks and Recreation website. For a topographic area map, request Rowe from USGS Map Sales, Federal Center, Box 25286, Denver, CO 80225, 888/ASK-USGS (888/275-8747), website: http://mapping.usgs.gov.

Directions

From MA 2, 1.6 miles west of the junction of Routes 2 and 8A in Charlemont and 2.1 miles east of the Mohawk Trail State Forest entrance, turn right at the Rowe/Monroe sign. Proceed 2.2 miles, bear left, and continue another 0.8 mile to the Zoar picnic area on the left, where there is parking, or to parking 0.1 mile farther on the right, immediately before the bridge over Deerfield River.

Contact

Mohawk Trail State Forest, P.O. Box 7, MA 2, Charlemont, MA 01339, 413/339-5504. Massachusetts Division of State Parks and Recreation, 251 Causeway Street, Suite 600, Boston, MA 02114-2104, 617/626-1250, website: www.state.ma.us/dem/forparks.htm.

12 THE LOOKOUT
in Mohawk Trail State Forest in Charlemont

Total distance: 2.2 miles round-trip   **Hiking time:** 1.5 hours

Difficulty: 2   **Rating:** 7

Here's an easy 2.2-mile walk through the quiet woods of Mohawk Trail State Forest to a lookout with a good view east toward the Deerfield River Valley and Charlemont. Some friends
and I encountered a ruffed grouse on this trail one snowless
March day. From the parking area, cross the Route to the
Totem Trail, which begins behind a stone marker for the state
forest. The trail is obvious and well marked, crossing a small
brook and reaching the overlook in 1.1 miles. Hike back along
the same route. This hike climbs about 600 feet.

User Groups
Hikers, snowshoers, and dogs. Dogs must be leashed. No wheel-
chair facilities. The trail is not suitable for bikes, horses, or skis.
Hunting is allowed in season.

Access and Fees
A daily parking fee of $5 is collected from mid-May to mid-Octo-
ber at some trailheads.

Maps
A free, basic trail and contour map of Mohawk Trail State Forest is available at the state forest headquarters or at the Massachusetts Division of State Parks and Recreation website. For a
topographic area map, request Rowe from USGS Map Sales,
Federal Center, Box 25286, Denver, CO 80225, 888/ASK-USGS
(888/275-8747), website: http://mapping.usgs.gov.

Directions
The trail begins opposite a turnout and picnic area on MA 2 in
Charlemont, 0.9 mile west of the Mohawk Trail State Forest
main entrance and 0.1 mile east of the Charlemont/Savoy line.

Contact

Mohawk Trail State Forest, P.O. Box 7, MA 2, Charlemont, MA 01339, 413/339-5504. Massachusetts Division of State Parks and Recreation, 251 Causeway Street, Suite 600, Boston, MA 02114-2104, 617/626-1250, website: www.state.ma.us/dem/forparks.htm.

13 FIRE TOWER HIKE
in D.A.R. State Forest in Goshen

Total distance: 3 miles round-trip   **Hiking time:** 2 hours

Difficulty: 3   **Rating:** 7

This 1,500-acre state forest has a network of fun forest roads for mountain biking or cross-country skiing, hiking trails through interesting woodlands, and a hilltop fire tower that affords 360-degree views of the countryside. (See next two listings for other possibilities.) This hike follows the Long Trail (not to be confused with the trail running the length of Vermont), which begins between the boat launch and the night registration office and makes a circuitous route of about 1.5 miles through the state forest to the fire tower. Climbing the tower's steps, you get a panorama of the surrounding countryside, with views stretching to Mount Monadnock to the northeast, the Holyoke Range and Mount Tom to the southeast, and Mount Greylock to the northwest. Descend the same way you hiked up.

User Groups
Hikers, snowshoers, and dogs. Dogs must be leashed. No wheelchair facilities. This trail is not suitable for bikes, horses, or skis. Hunting is prohibited.

Access and Fees
A daily parking fee of $5 is collected from mid-May to mid-October.

Maps
A free trail map is available at the state forest or at the Massachusetts Division of State Parks and Recreation website.

Directions
From I-91 northbound, take Exit 19 onto Route 9 west. In Goshen, turn right onto Route 112 north. The park entrance is on your right. From I-91 southbound, take Exit 25 for Route 116 west. In Ashfield, turn left onto Route 112 south. The park entrance is on your left. In summer, park in the second lot along Moore Hill Road, located just past the left turn for the boat

launch and nature center. In winter, park in the first lot, near the restrooms and warming hut (Moore Hill Road is not maintained beyond that point).

Contact

D.A.R. State Forest, Route 112, Goshen, MA, 413/268-7098; or mail to 555 East Street, RFD 1, Williamsburg, MA 01096. Massachusetts Division of State Parks and Recreation, 251 Causeway Street, Suite 600, Boston, MA 02114-2104, 617/626-1250, website: www.state.ma.us/dem/forparks.htm.

14 D.A.R. STATE FOREST SKI TOURING LOOP
in D.A.R. State Forest in Goshen

Total distance: 6 miles round-trip   **Hiking time:** 3.5 hours

Difficulty: 4   **Rating:** 7

I've included this loop for cross-country skiers looking for a moderate ski tour and a nice view from a fire tower. The approximately six-mile route largely follows state forest roads that are not maintained in winter; a friend and I skied this one winter when we could not find snow in much of Massachusetts and southern New Hampshire, and we found plenty of it in D.A.R. State Forest. From spring through fall, the road that this route follows is maintained for vehicular traffic; the better choice for a hike during that time would be the Fire Tower Hike (see previous listing).

Head out from the first parking lot on Moore Hill Road, ascending to the fire tower; a sign directs you to it. If you climb the tower's steps, you enjoy a panorama of the surrounding countryside, with views stretching to New Hampshire's Mount Monadnock to the northeast, the Holyoke Range and Mount Tom to the southeast, and Mount Greylock to the northwest. Backtrack from the tower, but before reaching Moore Hill Road, turn right onto another woods road, Oak Hill Road, which descends steeply to a junction with Wing Hollow Road. Turn left and continue until you reach pavement; carry your skis about a quarter mile, turn left onto Moore Hill Road, and take the long climb back over the hill and down to the parking area. You could also combine this with the hike to Balancing Rock, though short trail sections might be difficult on skis (we skied out there and had a ball, though). Don't expect many signs marking roads or trails.

User Groups
Hikers, bikers, dogs, horses, skiers, and snowshoers. Dogs must be leashed. No wheelchair facilities. Hunting is prohibited.

Access and Fees
A daily parking fee of $5 is collected from mid-May to mid-October.

Maps

A free trail map is available at the state forest or at the Massachusetts Division of State Parks and Recreation website.

Directions

From I-91 northbound, take Exit 19 onto Route 9 west. In Goshen, turn right onto Route 112 north. The park entrance is on your right. From I-91 southbound, take Exit 25 for Route 116 west. In Ashfield, turn left onto Route 112 south. The park entrance is on your left. In summer, park in the second lot along Moore Hill Road, located just past the left turn for the boat launch and nature center. In winter, park in the first lot, near the restrooms and warming hut (Moore Hill Road is not maintained beyond that point).

Contact

D.A.R. State Forest, Route 112, Goshen, MA, 413/268-7098; or mail to 555 East Street, RFD 1, Williamsburg, MA 01096. Massachusetts Division of State Parks and Recreation, 251 Causeway Street, Suite 600, Boston, MA 02114-2104, 617/626-1250, website: www.state.ma.us/dem/forparks.htm.

15 BALANCING ROCK
in D.A.R. State Forest in Goshen
Total distance: 1 mile round-trip   **Hiking time:** 0.75 hour

Difficulty: 2   **Rating:** 7

Here is a hike of about one mile that is both worthwhile and easy—even for young children—leading to an interesting glacial erratic out in the woods. A friend and I skied these trails to find the boulder wearing a cap of white one winter afternoon.

Head south along the woods road opposite the second parking lot, following the blue blazes. At the intersection of several trails, turn left onto the trail with orange blazes and follow it all the way to Balancing Rock, a truck-size boulder in the woods. Continue to follow the orange blazes past Balancing Rock, paralleling a stone wall at one point, back to a wide trail in the dark woods where you'll turn right and return shortly to the start of the orange-blazed trail. At this point, turn left on the blue-blazed trail back to the parking lot.

User Groups
Hikers, dogs, skiers, and snowshoers. Dogs must be leashed. No wheelchair facilities. This trail is not suitable for horses. Hunting is prohibited.

Access and Fees
A daily parking fee of $5 is collected from mid-May to mid-October.

Maps
A free trail map is available at the state forest or at the Massachusetts Division of State Parks and Recreation website.

Directions
From I-91 northbound, take Exit 19 onto Route 9 west. In Goshen, turn right onto Route 112 north. The park entrance is on your right. From I-91 southbound, take Exit 25 for Route 116 west. In Ashfield, turn left onto Route 112 south. The park entrance is on your left. In summer, park in the second lot along Moore Hill Road, located just past the left turn for the boat

launch and nature center. In winter, park in the first lot, near the restrooms and warming hut (Moore Hill Road is not maintained beyond that point).

Contact

D.A.R. State Forest, Route 112, Goshen, MA, 413/268-7098; or mail to 555 East Street, RFD 1, Williamsburg, MA 01096. Massachusetts Division of State Parks and Recreation, 251 Causeway Street, Suite 600, Boston, MA 02114-2104, 617/626-1250, website: www.state.ma.us/dem/forparks.htm.

16 SOUTH SUGARLOAF MOUNTAIN

in Mount Sugarloaf State Reservation in South Deerfield

Total distance: 1.5 miles round-trip   **Hiking time:** 1.5 hours

Difficulty: 2   **Rating:** 8

At just 652 feet above sea level, South Sugarloaf is barely a hill—but one that rises abruptly from the flat valley, its cliffs looming over the wide Connecticut River. Reached via this short but steep hike, the South Sugarloaf summit offers some of the best Massachusetts views of the Connecticut Valley. The vertical ascent is about 300 feet.

From the parking lot, the wide (though unmarked) West Side Trail leads into the woods. A side trail branches right immediately, soon leading across the Summit Road to the start of the Pocumtuck Ridge Trail, marked by a wooden post without a sign. (The Pocumtuck Ridge Trail can also be reached by walking up the Summit Road about 100 feet inside the gate.) Follow the blue blazes straight up the steep hillside under power lines; the trail finally makes several switchbacks just below the summit. It follows the fence edge, with sweeping views from atop the cliffs. An observation tower on the summit provides a panorama.

Cross the summit to the lower parking lot, where the blue-blazed Pocumtuck Ridge Trail reenters the woods and follows the clifftop, descending steeply and passing a fenced overlook. After crossing the Summit Road's hairpin turn, descend an old woods road to where the trail forks and turn left onto the sporadically red-blazed West

looking down on the Connecticut River Valley from South Sugarloaf Mountain

Side Trail. Just before reaching a dead-end paved road, the trail turns left, skirting the edges of fields and returning to the parking lot. If hiking a loop isn't important to you, go up the West Side Trail and the Pocumtuck Ridge Trail to the summit and return the same way; though somewhat longer, it's a more pleasant hike than the lower stretch of the Pocumtuck Ridge Trail.

User Groups

Hikers and dogs. Dogs must be leashed. No wheelchair facilities. This trail would be difficult to snowshoe, and is not suitable for bikes, horses, or skis. Hunting is prohibited.

Access and Fees

A daily parking fee of $2 is collected from mid-May to mid-October.

Maps

For a free, basic map of hiking trails, contact the Mount Sugarloaf State Reservation or see the Massachusetts Division of State Parks and Recreation website. *The Mount Toby Reservation Trail Map,* which covers the Mount Sugarloaf State Reservation, is $3.95 from New England Cartographics, 413/549-4124 or toll-free 888/995-6277, website: www.necartographics.com. For a topographic area map, request Williamsburg from USGS Map Sales, Federal Center, Box 25286, Denver, CO 80225, 888/ASK-USGS (888/275-8747), website: http://mapping.usgs.gov.

Directions

From the junction of Routes 47 and 116 in Sunderland, drive 0.7 mile west on Route 116 and turn right onto Sugarloaf Road. The Mount Sugarloaf State Reservation Summit Road begins immediately on the right; park in the dirt lot along Sugarloaf Road just beyond the turn for the Summit Road.

Contact

Mount Sugarloaf State Reservation, Sugarloaf Street/Route 116, South Deerfield, MA 01373, 413/545-5993. Massachusetts Division of State Parks and Recreation, 251 Causeway Street, Suite 600, Boston, MA 02114-2104, 617/626-1250, website: www.state.ma.us/dem/forparks.htm.

17 MOUNT TOBY
in Sunderland

Total distance: 5 miles round-trip   **Hiking time:** 2.5 hours

Difficulty: 6   **Rating:** 7

The well-maintained Summit Road provides a route to the top of Mount Toby that can be hiked easily—or biked or skied by anyone seeking a fairly challenging climb and a fast descent. The hike described here ascends the Summit Road but descends the steeper Telephone Line Trail to complete a loop; skiers or bikers should double back at the top and descend the Summit Road instead. Toby's 1,269-foot summit is wooded, but a fire tower open to the public offers a panorama with views stretching 50 miles across five states on a clear day. This hike climbs about 800 feet in elevation.

The Summit Road begins behind the Mount Toby Forest sign (don't turn right onto the orange-blazed Robert Frost Trail, although that is an alternate route). Frequent white blazes begin a short distance down the road. After less than a mile, the Telephone Line Trail (which you'll follow on the descent) diverges right. Approaching the summit, the road coincides with the orange-blazed Robert Frost Trail. From the fire tower, follow the Telephone Line Trail down Mount Toby. The Telephone Line Trail eventually reaches the Summit Road near the start of the hike; turn left and follow the Summit Road back to the trailhead. Another option for the return trip is to pick up the Robert Frost Trail, which diverges left about halfway down the Telephone Line Trail and also leads back to the Summit Road start.

User Groups
Hikers, snowshoers, and dogs. Dogs must be leashed. No wheelchair facilities. Parts of the trail are not suitable for bikes, horses, or skis, but Summit Road is open to them (see the trail notes above). Hunting is allowed in season.

Access and Fees
Parking and access are free.

Maps

The Mount Toby Reservation Trail Map is $3.95 from New England Cartographics, 413/549-4124 or toll-free 888/995-6277, website: www.necartographics.com. For topographic area maps, request Greenfield and Williamsburg from USGS Map Sales, Federal Center, Box 25286, Denver, CO 80225, 888/ASK-USGS (888/275-8747), website: http://mapping.usgs.gov.

Directions

The Mount Toby Summit Road is off Reservation Road, which comes off Route 47 0.9 mile south of its junction with Route 63 and just north of the Sunderland town line (there may not be a sign for Reservation Road). Follow it for 0.5 mile and park in a dirt lot on the right, just past the sign for the Mount Toby Forest.

Contact

Mount Toby Reservation is owned by the University of Massachusetts, but there is no contact for this hike.

18 MONUMENT MOUNTAIN
in Great Barrington

Total distance: 1.6 miles round-trip   **Hiking time:** 1.2 hours

Difficulty: 2   **Rating:** 10

Perhaps the finest hike in an area that rivals the Mount Greylock region for the best hiking in southern New England, Monument Mountain thrusts a spectacular gray-white quartzite ridge into the sky. Its summit, Squaw Peak, rises to 1,640 feet and offers three-state views in all directions. Arguably even more dramatic, though, are the cliffs south of Squaw Peak and the detached rock pinnacle known as Devil's Pulpit. A good time to come here is mid-June, when the mountain laurel blooms. This unique hill has been popular since at least the 19th century: In 1850, so legend goes, Nathaniel Hawthorne, Oliver Wendell Holmes, and Herman Melville picnicked together on Monument's summit. And William Cullen Bryant wrote a poem titled "Monument Moun-

on Monument Mountain

tain" relating the tale of an Indian maiden who, spurned in love, leapt to her death from the cliffs. Your hike may be less historic and less traumatic than either of those, but Monument Mountain is one not to miss.

This fairly easy, 1.6-mile hike ascends and descends the Hickey Trail, but you may enjoy making a loop hike, going up the Hickey and coming down the 1.3-mile Indian Monument Trail, which joins up with the Hickey below the summit. At the picnic area, a sign describes the trail heading south, the Indian Monument, as easier, and the Hickey, which heads north, as steeper. The Hickey actually grows steep for only a short section below the summit and is otherwise a well-graded and well-maintained trail. Following the white blazes, you parallel a brook with a small waterfall. Nearing the summit ridge, watch for a trail entering on the right; that's the Indian Monument Trail, and you want to be able to distinguish it from the Hickey on your way back down. From the summit, continue following the white blazes south about a quarter mile, passing a pile of rocks, until you reach the cliffs. Devil's Pulpit is the obvious pinnacle at the far end of the cliffs.

User Groups

Hikers and snowshoers. No wheelchair facilities. Bikes, dogs, horses, hunting, and skis are prohibited.

Access and Fees

Parking and access are free. Monument Mountain is open to the public from sunrise to sunset year-round.

Maps

A map of trails is posted on an information board at the picnic area, and a paper map is available at the trailhead. A map is also available from The Trustees of Reservations. For topographic area maps, request Great Barrington and Stockbridge from USGS Map Sales, Federal Center, Box 25286, Denver, CO 80225, 888/ASK-USGS (888/275-8747), website: http://mapping.usgs.gov.

Directions

The trails begin at a large turnout and picnic area along Route 7 in Great Barrington, 1.1 miles south of the Stockbridge town line and 1.7 miles north of the junction with Route 183.

Contact

The Trustees of Reservations Western Management Region, Mission House, P.O. Box 792, Sergeant Street, Stockbridge, MA 01262-0792, 413/298-3239, website: www.thetrustees.org.

19 WILDCAT LOOP
in Beartown State Forest in Monterey

Total distance: 9.5 miles round-trip   **Hiking time:** 6 hours

Difficulty: 6   **Rating:** 7

I included this trail primarily for mountain bikers looking for a challenging bounce up and down a heavily rutted and rock-strewn old woods road (a 2.5-hour ride). I emerged from this ride covered with a thick paste of mud and sweat—and with a new-found respect for Beartown's hills. As a hike, it represents a rugged, six-hour outing through quiet woods, though it tends to get muddy in some spots.

From the campground, head up Beartown Road a short distance and turn left onto the Wildcat Trail, which is marked by a sign and is just beyond a right bend in the road. This old woods road rolls up and down a few hills, passing through areas that tend to be muddy, especially in spring. After about 3.5 miles, the trail reaches paved Beartown Road. Turn right, cross over West Brook, and turn left onto Beebe Trail, another woods road marked by a sign. The Beebe loops less than two miles back to Beartown Road. Turn left and follow the paved road back to the campground. For a longer route, you can link up with the Sky Peak and Turkey Trails, both of which are clearly labeled on the map.

User Groups
Hikers, bikers, snowshoes, skis, and dogs. Dogs must be leashed. No wheelchair facilities. Horses are prohibited. Hunting is allowed in season.

Access and Fees
A daily parking fee of $5 is collected from mid-May to mid-October. Beartown State Forest is closed from dusk to a half hour before sunrise year-round.

Maps
A contour map of trails (designating uses allowed on each trail) is available in boxes at the state forest headquarters, at the parking area for hiking, at a trail information kiosk at the swimming

area and restrooms, and at the campground. You can also find one at the Massachusetts Division of State Parks and Recreation website. For topographic area maps, request Great Barrington and Otis from USGS Map Sales, Federal Center, Box 25286, Denver, CO 80225, 888/ASK-USGS (888/275-8747), website: http://mapping.usgs.gov.

Directions

Beartown State Forest is on Blue Hill Road, which runs north off Route 23, 2.4 miles west of the Monterey General Store and 1.8 miles east of the junction with Route 57. Follow Blue Hill Road 0.7 mile to the forest headquarters on the left. Continuing north on Blue Hill Road, you pass the Appalachian Trail crossing at 1.3 miles from the headquarters; at 1.5 miles, turn right onto Benedict Pond Road (shown as Beartown Road on the park map). Follow signs past the hiking trailhead and swimming area to the campground parking area.

Contact

Beartown State Forest, 69 Blue Hill Road, P.O. Box 97, Monterey, MA 01245-0097, 413/528-0904. Massachusetts Division of State Parks and Recreation, 251 Causeway Street, Suite 600, Boston, MA 02114-2104, 617/626-1250, website: www.state.ma.us/dem/forparks.htm.

20 BENEDICT POND AND THE LEDGES

in Beartown State Forest in Monterey

Total distance: 2.5 miles round-trip   **Hiking time:** 1.5 hours

Difficulty: 2   **Rating:** 8

This hike makes a loop around pristine Benedict Pond, a place with rich bird life—I heard three or four woodpeckers hard at work one morning and saw one fairly close up. When I stopped to eat by the pond's shore, a pair of Canada geese with two goslings in tow swam up and waddled ashore not eight feet from me as I sat quietly; the gander stood sentry over me while his family grazed on grass.

From the trailhead, follow the Pond Loop Trail to the pond's eastern end, where it merges with the white-blazed Appalachian Trail. Turn left. The trails soon reach a woods road and split again. Turn right onto the Appalachian Trail, ascending a low hillside. Where the Appalachian Trail hooks right and crosses a brook, continue straight ahead on a short side path to an impressive beaver dam that has flooded a swamp. Backtrack, cross the brook on the Appalachian Trail, and within several minutes you reach The Ledges, with a view west toward East Mountain and Mount Everett. Backtrack on the Appalachian Trail to the woods road and turn right onto the Pond Loop Trail. Watch for where the trail bears left off the woods road (at a sign and blue blazes). The trail passes through the state forest campground on the way back to the parking area.

User Groups

Hikers, snowshoers, and dogs. Dogs must be leashed. No wheelchair facilities. Bikes, horses, and skis are prohibited. Hunting is allowed in season.

Access and Fees

A daily parking fee of $5 is collected from mid-May to mid-October. Beartown State Forest is closed from dusk to a half hour before sunrise year-round.

Maps

A contour map of trails (designating uses allowed on each trail)

is available in boxes at the state forest headquarters, at the trail-head parking area, at a trail information kiosk at the swimming area and restrooms, and at the campground. You can also find one at the Massachusetts Division of State Parks and Recreation website. This Appalachian Trail section is covered on map 3 in the *Map and Guide to the Appalachian Trail in Massachusetts and Connecticut,* a five-map set for $19.95 ($14.95 for the maps alone) from the Appalachian Trail Conference. For topographic area maps, request Great Barrington and Otis from USGS Map Sales, Federal Center, Box 25286, Denver, CO 80225, 888/ASK-USGS (888/275-8747), website: http://mapping.usgs.gov.

Directions

Beartown State Forest is on Blue Hill Road, which runs north off Route 23, 2.4 miles west of the Monterey General Store and 1.8 miles east of the junction with Route 57. Follow Blue Hill Road 0.7 mile to the forest headquarters on the left. Continuing north on Blue Hill Road, you pass the Appalachian Trail crossing 1.3 miles from the headquarters; at 1.5 miles, turn right onto Benedict Pond Road (shown as Beartown Road on the park map). Follow signs to the trailhead in a dirt parking area; a sign marks the Pond Loop Trail. A short distance farther up the road are public restrooms and a state forest campground.

Contact

Beartown State Forest, Blue Hill Road, P.O. Box 97, Monterey, MA 01245-0097, 413/528-0904. Massachusetts Division of State Parks and Recreation, 251 Causeway Street, Suite 600, Boston, MA 02114-2104, 617/626-1250, website: www.state.ma.us/dem/forparks.htm. Appalachian Trail Conference, P.O. Box 807, Harpers Ferry, WV 25425, 304/535-6331, website: www.appalachiantrail.org.

21 NORWOTTUCK TRAIL
in Northampton

Total distance: 10.1 miles one-way   **Hiking time:** 5 hours

Difficulty: 4   **Rating:** 7

The 10.1-mile-long Norwottuck Trail is a paved bike path that follows a former railroad bed from Northampton, through Hadley and Amherst, into Belchertown. Its flat course provides a linear recreation area for walkers, runners, bicyclists, in-line skaters, cross-country skiers, snowshoers, and people in wheelchairs. As with any bike or pedestrian path, it is popular with families because it provides a refuge from traffic. The place from which many users access the trail is the large parking lot at its western end; this lot is often full, so it's wise to try one of the other access points among those listed below in the directions. Park officials are hoping to eventually complete an extension of the Norwottuck to Woodmont Road in Northampton, or possibly as far as the University of Massachusetts campus in Amherst.

User Groups
Hikers, bikers, dogs, skiers, snowshoers, and wheelchair users. Dogs must be leashed. Horses and hunting are prohibited.

Access and Fees
Parking and access are free.

Maps
A brochure/map is available at both trailheads. The *Western Massachusetts Bicycle Map,* a detailed bicycling map covering the state from the New York border to the Quabbin Reservoir, including the Norwottuck Trail, is available for $4.25 from Rubel BikeMaps, P.O. Box 401035, Cambridge, MA 02140, 617/776-6567, website: www.bikemaps.com, and from area stores listed at the website. For topographic area maps, request Easthampton and Holyoke from USGS Map Sales, Federal Center, Box 25286, Denver, CO 80225, 888/ASK-USGS (888/275-8747), website: http://mapping.usgs.gov.

Directions

To reach the trail's western end from the south, take I-91 to Exit 19. Down the off-ramp, drive straight through the intersection and turn right into the Connecticut River Greenway State Park/Elwell Recreation Area. From the north, take I-91 to Exit 20. Turn left at the traffic lights and drive 1.5 miles to the Elwell Recreation Area on the left. The trail can also be accessed from four other parking areas: behind the Bread and Circus store in the Mountain Farms Mall on Route 9 in Hadley, 3.7 miles from the Elwell Recreation Area parking lot; near the junction of Mill Lane and Southeast Street, off Route 9 in Amherst; on Station Road in Amherst (reached via Southeast Street off Route 9), 1.6 miles from the trail's eastern terminus; and on Warren Wright Road in Belchertown, the trail's eastern terminus.

Contact

Connecticut River Greenway State Park/Elwell Recreation Area, 136 Damon Road, Northampton, MA 01060, 413/586-8706, ext. 12. Massachusetts Division of State Parks and Recreation, 251 Causeway Street, Suite 600, Boston, MA 02114-2104, 617/626-1250, website: www.state.ma.us/dem/forparks.htm.

22 MOUNT TOM
in Mount Tom State Reservation in Holyoke

Total distance: 5.4 miles round-trip   **Hiking time:** 2.5 hours

Difficulty: 4   **Rating:** 8

One of the most popular stretches of the 98-mile Metacomet-Monadnock Trail is the traverse of the Mount Tom Ridge. A steep mountainside capped by tall basalt cliffs defines Mount Tom's west face, and the trail follows the brink of that precipice for nearly two miles, treating hikers to commanding views west as far as the Berkshires on a clear day. This hike climbs less than 500 feet.

From the parking area, walk up the paved road toward the stone house for about 75 yards. Turn right and enter the woods at a trail marked by white rectangular blazes and a triangular marker for the Metacomet-Monadnock Trail. Within minutes, the trail veers right and climbs steeply toward Goat Peak. Pass a good view westward and then reach the open clearing of Goat Peak, where the lookout tower offers a panorama. Double back to Smiths Ferry Road, turn right, walk about 75 yards, and then enter the woods on the left, following the white blazes of the Metacomet-Monadnock. It crosses the Quarry Trail and then ascends the ridge. Numerous side paths lead to the right to great views from the cliffs, with each view better than the last until you reach the Mount Tom summit, where there are radio and television transmission stations. Retrace your steps on the Metacomet-Monadnock Trail to your car.

User Groups
Hikers and snowshoers. Dogs must be leashed. No wheelchair facilities. This trail is not suitable for skis. Bikes, horses, and hunting are prohibited.

Access and Fees
A daily parking fee of $2 is collected from mid-May to mid-October.

Maps
A free map of hiking trails is available at the reservation headquarters and the stone house, or at the Massachusetts Division

of State Parks and Recreation website. The *Blue Hills Reservation/Mount Tom/Holyoke Range* map costs $5.95 in paper from the Appalachian Mountain Club, 800/262-4455, website: www.outdoors.org. The *Mount Tom Reservation Trail Map* costs $3.95 from New England Cartographics, 413/549-4124 or toll-free 888/995-6277, website: www.necartographics.com. For topographic area maps, request Mount Tom, Easthampton, Mount Holyoke, and Springfield North from USGS Map Sales, Federal Center, Box 25286, Denver, CO 80225, 888/ASK-USGS (888/275-8747), website: http://mapping.usgs.gov.

Directions

Take I-91 to Exit 18 and then U.S. 5 south for roughly 3.3 miles. Turn right onto Smiths Ferry Road, at the entrance to Mount Tom State Reservation. Follow the road for nearly a mile, passing under I-91 (immediately after which the reservation headquarters are on the right), to a horseshoe-shaped parking area on the right. The parking area is about 0.2 mile before the stone house interpretive center, where Smiths Ferry Road meets Christopher Clark Road, just beyond a paved, dead-end road.

Contact

Mount Tom State Reservation, 125 Reservation Road, Route 5, Holyoke, MA 01040, 413/534-1186. Massachusetts Division of State Parks and Recreation, 251 Causeway Street, Suite 600, Boston, MA 02114-2104, 617/626-1250, website: www.state.ma.us/dem/forparks.htm.

23 JUG END

in Egremont

Total distance: 2.2 miles round-trip

Hiking time: 2 hours

Difficulty: 2

Rating: 8

I hiked up to Jug End on a morning when a leaden sky threatened rain and clouds hung low on many of the bigger hills in this part of the southern Berkshires. I considered not even making the hike of barely more than two miles—but ultimately went up and encountered some exciting conditions. At the summit, I stood in an icy wind watching low clouds drift across the valley between rounded mountains. The view from the open ledges above cliffs at Jug End is well worth the short, if steep, hike of more than 500 feet uphill.

From the turnout, follow the Appalachian Trail steeply uphill. Within 0.3 mile, the trail starts up the steep ridge side, reaching the first open views at about 0.7 mile from the road. Jug End's summit, with good views northward toward the valley and the surrounding green hills of the southern Berkshires, is 1.1 miles from the road. After you've taken in the views, head back to the parking area the same way you hiked up.

User Groups

Hikers, snowshoers, and dogs. No wheelchair facilities. This trail is not suitable for skis. Bikes, horses, and hunting are prohibited.

Access and Fees

Parking and access are free.

Maps

Refer to map 3 in the *Map and Guide to the Appalachian Trail in Massachusetts and Connecticut,* a five-map set and guidebook available for $19.95 ($14.95 for the maps alone) from the Appalachian Trail Conference. For topographic area maps, request Ashley Falls and Great Barrington from USGS Map Sales, Federal Center, Box 25286, Denver, CO 80225, 888/ASK-USGS (888/275-8747), website: http://mapping.usgs.gov.

Directions

From the junction of Routes 23 and 41 in Egremont, drive south on Route 41 for 0.1 mile and turn right onto Mount Washington Road. Continue 0.8 mile and turn left on Avenue Road. At 0.5 mile, bear left onto Jug End Road and continue 0.3 mile to a turnout on the right where the Appalachian Trail emerges from the woods. Park in the turnout.

Contact

Appalachian Trail Conference, 799 Washington Street, P.O. Box 807, Harpers Ferry, WV 25425-0807, 304/535-6331, website: www.appalachiantrail.org.

24 MOUNT EVERETT

in Mount Washington

Total distance: 5.4 miles round-trip   **Hiking time:** 3.5 hours

Difficulty: 7   **Rating:** 8

Mount Everett, at 2,602 feet, is among the taller of those little hills in southwestern Massachusetts with the green, rounded tops and steep flanks that seem close enough for someone standing in the valley to reach out and touch. Long views east from atop Everett suggest that it's a good place to catch the sunrise. As a bonus, you pass several waterfalls on the way to the peak. This hike climbs about 1,900 feet.

From the kiosk, follow the Race Brook Trail. Not far up the trail, a sign marks a side path leading right to a view of the lower falls along Race Brook. The main trail bears left and grows steeper just before crossing the brook below upper Race Brook Falls, some 80 feet high—an impressive sight at times of high runoff, most common in the spring. Above the falls, you reach a ledge with a view east. The trail then descends slightly to a third crossing of the brook.

At the Appalachian Trail, marked by signs, turn right (north)

hiking Mount Everett

for the summit of Everett, 0.7 mile distant. You are walking on bare rock exposed by the footsteps of the many hikers who have come before you—hundreds of whom were backpacking the entire Appalachian Trail from Georgia to Maine. Notice how thin the soil is beside the trail and you will understand how hiker traffic has eroded soil on the trail. The views eastward begin before the summit, where only stunted trees and vegetation grow; in this rural southwest corner of Massachusetts, you survey the valley and an expanse of wooded hills with few signs of human presence. An abandoned fire tower marks the summit; walk toward it to a spot with views toward the Catskills. Hike down along the same route.

User Groups
Hikers, snowshoers, and dogs. No wheelchair facilities. This trail is not suitable for skis. Bikes, horses, and hunting are prohibited.

Access and Fees
Parking and access are free.

Maps
A free trail map of Mount Washington State Forest, which covers Mount Everett, is available at the state forest headquarters or at the Massachusetts Division of State Parks and Recreation website. The *Northern Berkshires/Southwestern Massachusetts/ Wachusett Mountain* map costs $5.95 in paper from the Appalachian Mountain Club, 800/262-4455, website: www.outdoors.org. These trails are also covered on map 4 in the *Map and Guide to the Appalachian Trail in Massachusetts and Connecticut,* a five-map set and guidebook available for $19.95 ($14.95 for the maps alone) from the Appalachian Trail Conference. For a topographic area map, request Ashley Falls from USGS Map Sales, Federal Center, Box 25286, Denver, CO 80225, 888/ASK-USGS (888/275-8747), website: http://mapping.usgs.gov.

Directions
From the junction where Routes 23 and 41 split in Egremont, follow Route 41 south for 5.2 miles to a turnout on the right. A kiosk and blue blazes mark the start of the Race Brook Trail.

Contact

Mount Washington State Forest, RD 3 East Street, Mount Washington, MA 01258, 413/528-0330. Massachusetts Division of State Parks and Recreation, 251 Causeway Street, Suite 600, Boston, MA 02114-2104, 617/626-1250, website: www.state.ma.us/dem/forparks.htm. Appalachian Trail Conference, 799 Washington Street, P.O. Box 807, Harpers Ferry, WV 25425-0807, 304/535-6331, website: www.appalachiantrail.org.

25 THE RIGA PLATEAU
between Egremont, MA, and Salisbury, CT

Total distance: 1 / miles round-trip   **Hiking time:** 2 days

Difficulty: 8   **Rating:** 9

This very popular Appalachian Trail stretch offers easy hiking along a low ridge with numerous long views of the green hills and rural countryside. In my opinion, it's the nicest stretch of the Appalachian Trail south of New Hampshire's Mount Moosilauke. Expect to see lots of day hikers and backpackers on warm weekends here, with shelters and camping areas tending to fill to overflowing. I backpacked this once midweek, though, when I saw just three other backpackers in two days and shared the Bear Rock Falls campsite with only a group of well-behaved teens. It was May, and the trail and woods had already dried out from spring, yet there were very few bugs and the temperature was quite mild. I fell in love with this section of the Appalachian Trail and can't wait to get back again. The cumulative elevation gained over the course of this hike is about 3,500 feet.

From the turnout on Jug End Road, follow the Appalachian Trail southbound. You follow the Appalachian Trail's white blazes for this entire hike. The trail ascends gently, then steeply through the woods to Jug End at 1.1 miles, the northern tip of the so-called Riga Plateau, with wide views northward to the Berkshire Mountains. On a clear day, Mount Greylock, the highest peak in Massachusetts, is visible in the distance. Now you're on the ridge, with only fairly easy climbs and dips ahead. The trail passes several open ledges on the Mount Bushnell ascent, reaching its 1,834-foot summit at 2.3 miles. Easy woods walking leads you into the Mount Everett State Reservation, crossing a road at 3.9 miles; a short distance to the right is Guilder Pond, the second-highest in Massachusetts. The trail steepens a bit to a fire tower at 4.3 miles, and Everett's summit (2,602 feet) at 4.6 miles, with views in all directions.

The Appalachian Trail descends off Everett at an easy slope and heads back into the woods, then climbs slightly to the open, rocky Race Mountain crown, 6.4 miles into this hike and 2,365 feet above the ocean. The trail follows the crest of cliffs with wide views northeast to southeast of the Housatonic Valley. At 8.1 miles, you pass near Bear Rock Falls (on the left) and its namesake camping area. Beyond here, the trail descends steadily, then a bit more steeply into the dark defile of Sages Ravine, another camping area at 9.5 miles, as the Appalachian Trail enters Connecticut.

The Appalachian Trail follows the ravine, then leaves it for the most strenuous part of this hike, the 1.4-mile climb to the 2,316-foot Bear Mountain summit, the highest peak in Connecticut—though not the highest point, which is actually on a slope of nearby Mount Frissell. On the way up Bear Mountain, you pass the Paradise Lane Trail at 10.3 miles into this hike. From the top of Bear, at 10.9 miles, the trail descends steadily, if easily, over open terrain with long views of Connecticut's northwestern corner before reentering the woods. The Undermountain Trail turns sharply left at 11.8 miles; continue straight ahead on the Appalachian Trail, soon passing the Brassie Brook, Ball Brook, and Riga camping areas (see the Access section for this hike). The forest along here is bright, and although trees block the views, you're on the ridge and it feels high. I once hiked this at night under a brilliant moon, seeing a sky riddled with stars overhead.

Stay southbound on the Appalachian Trail, soon climbing more steeply to reach the open ledges of the Lion's Head at 14.2 miles, with some of the hike's best views of a bucolic countryside, including the town of Salisbury and Prospect Mountain straight ahead. Double back a short distance from the Lion's Head ledges and descend on the Appalachian Trail, passing a junction with the Lion's Head Trail. The trail now descends at a steady grade through quiet woods, reaching the parking lot on Route 41 at 17 miles from Jug End Road.

User Groups

Hikers, snowshoers, and dogs. No wheelchair facilities. This trail is not suitable for skis. Bikes, horses, and hunting are prohibited.

Access and Fees

Parking and access are free. Camping is permitted only at designated shelters and campsites along this section of the Appalachian Trail. From north to south, they are: Glen Brook shelter, reached via a short side trail off the Appalachian Trail, 3.4 miles into this hike; a campsite 0.4 mile off the Appalachian Trail down the Race Brook Falls Trail, 5.3 miles into this hike; the Bear Rock Falls campsite, beside the Appalachian Trail at 8.1 miles; Sages Ravine at 9.9 miles; the Brassie Brook shelter and campsites at 12.3 miles; the Ball Brook campsite at 12.9 miles; the Riga camping area at 13.5 miles; and the Plateau campsite at 13.7 miles, a short distance from the hike's end. Campfires are prohibited from Bear Rock Falls campsite south to the Plateau campsite. Campers must cook with portable camp stoves.

Maps

See maps 3 and 4 in the *Map and Guide to the Appalachian Trail in Massachusetts and Connecticut,* a five-map set and guidebook available for $19.95 ($14.95 for the maps alone) from the Appalachian Trail Conference. For topographic area maps, request Great Barrington, Ashley Falls, and Sharon from USGS Map Sales, Federal Center, Box 25286, Denver, CO 80225, 888/ASK-USGS (888/275-8747), website: http://mapping.usgs.gov.

Directions

You need to shuttle two vehicles to make this one-way traverse. To hike north to south, as described here, leave one vehicle in the Appalachian Trail parking lot on Route 41 in Salisbury, CT, 0.8 mile north of the junction of Routes 44 and 41. To reach this hike's start, drive your second vehicle north on Route 41 to Egremont. Just before reaching Route 23, turn left onto Mount Washington Road. Continue 0.8 mile and turn left on Avenue Road. At 0.5 mile, bear to the left onto Jug End Road and continue 0.3 mile to a turnout on the right where the Appalachian Trail emerges from the woods. Park in the turnout.

Contact

Appalachian Trail Conference, 799 Washington Street, P.O. Box 807, Harpers Ferry, WV 25425-0807, 304/535-6331, website: www.appalachiantrail.org.

26 BASH BISH FALLS

in Bash Bish Falls State Park in Mount Washington

Total distance: 0.5 miles round-trip   **Hiking time:** 0.75 hour

Difficulty: 2   **Rating:** 10

After driving one of the most winding Massachusetts roads, you hike this short trail to what may be the state's most spectacular waterfall. The stream tumbles down through a vertical stack of giant boulders—splitting into twin columns of water around one huge, triangular block—then settles briefly in a clear, deep pool at the base of the falls before dropping in a foaming torrent through the water-carved rock walls of Bash Bish Gorge. The falls are, predictably, enhanced by spring rains and snowmelt and much thinner in fall. The Bash Bish Falls Trail is well marked with blue triangles, and a 0.25-mile walk downhill from the roadside turnout leads to the falls.

User Groups

Hikers, snowshoers, and dogs. Dogs must be leashed. No wheelchair facilities. This trail is not suitable for bikes, horses, or skis. Hunting is allowed in season.

Access and Fees

Parking and access are free.

Maps

Although no map is needed for this hike, a free area trail map is available at the Mount Washington State Forest headquarters or at

at the base of Bash Bish Falls

COURTESY OF THE BERKSHIRE VISITORS BUREAU

the Massachusetts Division of State Parks and Recreation website. This area is covered in the *Northern Berkshires/Southwestern Massachusetts/Wachusett Mountain* map, $5.95 in paper, available in many stores and from the Appalachian Mountain Club, 800/262-4455, website: www.outdoors.org. For a topographic area map, request Ashley Falls from USGS Map Sales, Federal Center, Box 25286, Denver, CO 80225, 888/ASK-USGS (888/275-8747), website: http://mapping.usgs.gov.

Directions

From the junction of Routes 23 and 41 in Egremont, drive south on Route 41 for 0.1 mile and turn right onto Mount Washington Road, which becomes East Street. Follow the signs several miles to Bash Bish Falls State Park and a turnout on the left. To reach the Mount Washington State Forest headquarters, follow the signs from East Street.

Contact

Mount Washington State Forest, RD 3 East Street, Mount Washington, MA 01258, 413/528-0330. Massachusetts Division of State Parks and Recreation, 251 Causeway Street, Suite 600, Boston, MA 02114-2104, 617/626-1250, website: www.state.ma.us/dem/forparks.htm.

27 ALANDER MOUNTAIN

in Mount Washington State Forest in Mount Washington

Total distance: 5.6 miles round-trip   **Hiking time:** 3 hours

Difficulty: 4   **Rating:** 9

Less than a mile from the New York border and a few miles from Connecticut, Alander Mountain (2,240 feet) has two broad, flat summits, the westernmost having the best views of the southern Berkshires and of the New York hills and farmland all the way to the Catskill Mountains. An open ridge running south from the summit offers sweeping views for a fairly easy climb (500 feet in elevation gain). I rode my mountain bike as far as I could up the Alander Mountain Trail one spring afternoon and then hiked to the summit. Dark storm clouds drifted over the hills to the east, and shafts of sunlight daubed bright splotches over the green mountainsides while hawks floated on thermals overhead. While this is a wonderful hike, I think biking or skiing as far as possible up the trail adds another dimension to this little adventure.

From the kiosk behind the headquarters, the Alander Mountain Trail gradually ascends a woods road for much of its distance, then narrows to a trail and grows steeper. Just past the cabin, a sign points left to the east loop and right to the west loop; both loops take just minutes to walk. The west loop offers great views to the north, east, and south; three old concrete blocks, probably the foundation of a former fire tower, sit at the summit. Continue over the summit on the white-blazed South Taconic Trail for views westward into New York. Turn back and descend the way you came.

Special note: By hiking northbound from Alander's summit on the scenic South Taconic Trail, you can reach Bash Bish Falls (see previous listing), then return to Alander, adding four miles round-trip to this hike's distance.

User Groups

Hikers, bikers, dogs, horses, skiers, and snowshoers. Dogs must be leashed. No wheelchair facilities. Hunting is allowed in season. During the winter, watch out for snowmobiles.

Access and Fees

Parking and access are free. Backcountry camping is available in the Mount Washington State Forest, at 15 wilderness campsites just off this trail at 1.5 miles from the trailhead, and in a cabin that sleeps six just below Alander's summit. The cabin (which has a wood-burning stove) and the campsites are filled on a first-come, first-served basis.

Maps

The *Northern Berkshires/Southwestern Massachusetts/Wachusett Mountain* map costs $5.95 in paper and is available in many stores and from the Appalachian Mountain Club, 800/262-4455, website: www.outdoors.org. A free map of Mount Washington State Forest is available at the state forest headquarters or at the Massachusetts Division of State Parks and Recreation website. For a topographic area map, request Ashley Falls from USGS Map Sales, Federal Center, Box 25286, Denver, CO 80225, 888/ASK-USGS (888/275-8747), website: http://mapping.usgs.gov.

Directions

From the junction of Routes 23 and 41 in Egremont, drive south on Route 41 for 0.1 mile and turn right onto Mount Washington Road, which becomes East Street. Follow the signs about nine miles to the Mount Washington State Forest headquarters on the right. The blue-blazed Alander Mountain Trail begins behind the headquarters.

Contact

Mount Washington State Forest, RD 3 East Street, Mount Washington, MA 01258, 413/528-0330. Massachusetts Division of State Parks and Recreation, 251 Causeway Street, Suite 600, Boston, MA 02114-2104, 617/626-1250, website: www.state.ma.us/dem/forparks.htm.

28 HUBBARD RIVER GORGE

in Granville State Forest in Granville

Total distance: 6 miles round-trip   **Hiking time:** 2.5 hours

Difficulty: 5   **Rating:** 9

This out-and-back hike features the highlight of this out-of-the-way state forest—the Hubbard River Gorge, which drops 450 feet over 2.5 miles through numerous falls. I've done this hike in winter, when ice made the going treacherous and beautiful in places, and in a spring rain and hailstorm when the river swelled with runoff.

From the dirt lot, backtrack over the bridge and turn right onto the paved road leading 0.5 mile to the now-closed Hubbard River Campground; the Hubbard River Trail begins at the road's end. Follow the trail, an old woods road marked by blue triangles bearing a hiker symbol, southeast along the Hubbard River. After turning briefly away from the river, the road hugs the rim of the spectacular gorge, passing many spots that afford views of the river. Follow the trail as far as you like, then turn around and return the same way. If you go all the way to an old woods road marked on the map as Hartland Hollow Road before turning back, the round-trip is six miles. If you'd like to see another area similar to the Hubbard River Gorge, turn left and hike upstream (north) along Hartland Hollow Road. Watch for the stream through the trees to your right; you'll discover a small

Hubbard River Gorge, Granville State Forest

gorge and pools in there within less than a half mile from the Hubbard River Trail.

Special note: If you want to cross-country ski elsewhere in the state forest, check out the short but scenic Beaver Pond Loop beyond the forest headquarters on West Hartland Road, or the loop from the headquarters on the CCC and Corduroy Trails. One last note: This quiet corner of Massachusetts is a wonderful area to drive through or, better yet, bicycle. The villages of Granville and West Granville are both on the National Register of Historic Districts.

User Groups

Hikers, bikers, dogs, skiers, and snowshoers. Dogs must be leashed. No wheelchair facilities. Sections of the trail would be difficult on a bike or skis and could be icy in winter. Horses are allowed. Hunting is allowed in season, except on Sundays or within 150 feet of a paved road or bike trail. Swimming in the Hubbard River is prohibited under penalty of fine.

Access and Fees

Parking and access are free.

Maps

A free map of hiking trails is available at the state forest headquarters or at the Massachusetts Division of State Parks and Recreation website. For a topographic area map, request Southwick from USGS Map Sales, Federal Center, Box 25286, Denver, CO 80225, 888/ASK-USGS (888/275-8747), website: http://mapping.usgs.gov.

Directions

From the junction of Routes 189 and 57, drive six miles west on Route 57 and turn left onto West Hartland Road. In another 0.6 mile, you pass a sign for the Granville State Forest; the rough dirt road heading left from that point is where this loop hike will emerge. Continue another 0.3 mile, cross the bridge over the Hubbard River, and park in the dirt lot on the left. The state forest headquarters is on West Hartland Road, 0.6 mile beyond the bridge.

Contact

Granville State Forest, 323 West Hartland Road, Granville, MA
01034, 413/357-6611. Massachusetts Division of State Parks and
Recreation, 251 Causeway Street, Suite 600, Boston, MA 02114-
2104, 617/626-1250, website: www.state.ma.us/dem/forparks.htm.

Chapter 2

© MICHAEL LANZA

Central Massachusetts

Central Massachusetts

This chapter covers central Massachusetts from the Connecticut River east to I-495, from Douglas in the south to Ashburnham in the north. The state's midsection is a rumpled blanket of rolling hills and thick forest with some low but craggy summits that rise above the trees to give long views, most notable among them Mount Holyoke, Wachusett Mountain, and Mount Watatic.

Beyond these hills, you will mostly find pleasant woods walks that are easy to moderately difficult and make for enjoyable outings of anywhere from an hour to half a day. Many of them are also quiet, uncrowded, and easy to reach. These hikes are great for beginners as well as serious hikers and backpackers trying to get their legs in shape for more strenuous trips elsewhere.

Central Massachusetts has two long-distance trails, both of which are largely used by day hikers. The Metacomet-

Monadnock Trail (Crag Mountain, Mount Holyoke) bounces along the Holyoke Range and through the hills of north-central Massachusetts on its 117-mile course from the Massachusetts/Connecticut line near Agawam and Southwick to the summit of Mount Monadnock in Jaffrey, New Hampshire. The Midstate Trail extends 92 miles from Douglas (on the Rhode Island border) to the New Hampshire line in Ashburnham. Significant stretches of both trails are on private land, so be aware of and respect any closures.

The trails in this chapter usually become free of snow sometime between mid-March and mid-April, though they often will be muddy for a few weeks after the snow melts. Many of the hikes in this chapter are in state parks and forests, where dogs must be leashed; horses are allowed in most state forests and parks, as is hunting in season.

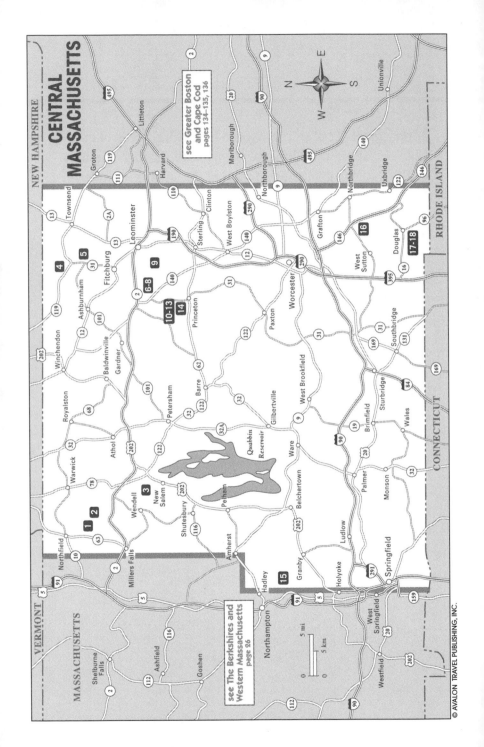

CENTRAL MASSACHUSETTS

NEW HAMPSHIRE

VERMONT

MASSACHUSETTS

RHODE ISLAND

CONNECTICUT

see Greater Boston
and Cape Cod
pages 134–135, 136

see The Berkshires and
Western Massachusetts
page 86

N
W   E
S

5 mi

5 km

© AVALON TRAVEL PUBLISHING, INC.

1 **2** **3** **4** **5** **6-8** **9** **10-13** **14** **15** **16** **17-18**

Contents

1 NORTHFIELD MOUNTAIN: ROSE LEDGE

in Northfield

Total distance: 5.5 miles round-trip   **Hiking time:** 3.5 hours

Difficulty: 6   **Rating:** 8

Owned by Northeast Utilities, the Northfield Mountain Recreation and Environmental Center's 25 miles of hiking and multi-use trails comprise one of the best trail systems open year-round in Massachusetts. The Metacomet-Monadnock Trail is not far from this system and can be reached via a marked trail off the 10th Mountain Trail, near Bugaboo Pass on Northfield Mountain. Other activities, including orienteering, canoeing on the nearby Connecticut River, and educational programs, are conducted through the center. This hike takes in some of the mountain's best features—including the Rose Ledge cliffs and a view of the reservoir at the 1,100-foot summit—but many other loop options are possible here. The route described here climbs about 600–700 feet in elevation.

From the parking lot, follow the wide carriage road of the 10th Mountain Trail to the right. At the sign, turn left onto a footpath, the Rose Ledge Trail (marked here by blue diamonds). Follow the trail across a carriage road and then turn right where the trail follows orange blazes. Cross two carriage roads, Hemlock Hill and Jug End. The Rose Ledge Trail forks here: The left branch traverses above the cliffs and the right branch below them. Either is a nice hike, and both branches link at the opposite end of the cliffs.

The left branch begins above the cliffs, with some views of nearby wooded hills, then drops below them for close-up views of the cliffs themselves. Bear left at the fork, and just before reaching the wide carriage road called Rock Oak Ramble, turn right at an easily overlooked trail leading downhill (parallel to Rock Oak Ramble). Reaching the Lower Ledge Trail, turn left and cross Rock Oak Ramble. You're soon walking below the cliffs and may see rock climbers on them; be careful of loose rock falling from above if you venture near the cliff base. After rejoining the Rose Ledge Trail, continue straight on the Mariah Foot Trail to the Hill 'n' Dale carriage road; turn right and then left onto the 10th Mountain carriage road. At a junction marked number 32 (corresponding to the trail map), turn right for the summit, which has a reservoir viewing platform. Descend back to Junction 32 and turn left on 10th Mountain, right on Hill 'n' Dale, right at Junction 16 onto Rock Oak Ramble, left at Junction 8 onto Hemlock Hill, and then right onto the orange-blazed Rose Ledge Trail, backtracking to the parking lot.

User Groups
Hikers, snowshoers, and dogs. Dogs must be leashed. No wheelchair facilities. Bikes, horses, hunting, and skis are prohibited from parts of this trail.

Access and Fees
No fee is charged for parking or trail use, with the exception of a trail fee for cross-country skiing. Bikers must register once per season at the visitors center, and horseback riders must check in for parking and trail information; helmets are required for both biking and horseback riding. Trails are often closed to bikes and horses during mud season, usually until late April.

Maps
A trail map is available at the visitors center. For topographic area maps, request Northfield and Orange from USGS Map Sales, Federal Center, Box 25286, Denver, CO 80225, 888/ASK-USGS (888/275-8747), website: http://mapping.usgs.gov.

Directions
The Northfield Mountain Visitor Center is off Route 63, 5.8 miles south of its junction with Route 10 and 2.5 miles north of Route 2. The visitors center is open 9 A.M.–5 P.M. Wednesday–Sunday, in the spring, summer, and fall. The cross-country center is open 9 A.M.–5 P.M. every day during the ski season.

Contact
Northfield Mountain Recreation and Environmental Center, 99 Millers Falls Road/Route 63, Northfield, MA 01360, 413/659-3714, website: www.tiac.com/users/erving/cyber/skiing.html.

2 CRAG MOUNTAIN
in Northfield

Total distance: 3.4 miles round-trip

Difficulty: 3

Hiking time: 2 hours

Rating: 9

This easy hike—ascending only a few hundred feet—leads to a rocky outcropping with excellent views. Follow the Metacomet-Monadnock Trail south. The trail crosses one wet area, rises gently through a forest, and reaches Crag's open summit in 1.7 miles. The views take in the Berkshires and the southern Green Mountains to the west and northwest, Mount Monadnock in New Hampshire to the northeast, the central Massachusetts hills to the east, and the Northfield Mountain Reservoir, Mount Toby (see listing in The Berkshires and Western Massachusetts chapter), and South Sugarloaf Mountain (see listing in The Berkshires and Western Massachusetts chapter) to the south. Hike back along the same route.

User Groups
Hikers, snowshoers, and dogs. No wheelchair facilities. The trail is not suitable for bikes, horses, or skis. This hike is on private land; assume that hunting is allowed unless otherwise posted.

Access and Fees
Parking and access are free.

Maps
For a topographic area map, request Northfield from USGS Map Sales, Federal Center, Box 25286, Denver, CO 80225, 888/ASK-USGS (888/275-8747), website: http://mapping.usgs.gov.

Directions
From Route 10/63 in Northfield, about 0.2 mile south of the town center and 0.3 mile north of the southern junction of Routes 10 and 63, turn west onto Maple Street, which becomes Gulf Road. Drive 3.1 miles to a turnout on the right, where the white blazes of the Metacomet-Monadnock Trail enter the woods.

Contact
There is no contact organization for this hike.

3 BEAR'S DEN
in New Salem

Total distance: 0.2 miles round-trip   **Hiking time:** 0.5 hour

Difficulty: 1   **Rating:** 7

This compact but dramatic gorge along the Middle Branch of the Swift River is a beautiful spot just a few minutes from the road. At the trailhead, follow the left fork of the trail to reach the gorge rim, where you can stand at the brink of a precipitous drop to the river. Double back and follow the trail downhill to the banks of the river, where the foundations of an old grist mill still stand. A sign near the trail's beginning relates some of this spot's history: how a settler killed a black bear here, thus explaining the name Bear's Den, and how the Wampanoag Indian chief King Phillip supposedly met with other chiefs here in 1675 during their wars with European settlers in the Connecticut Valley.

User Groups
Hikers, snowshoers, and dogs. No wheelchair facilities. This trail is not suitable for bikes, horses, or skis. Hunting is prohibited.

Access and Fees
Parking and access are free. The reservation is open to the public from sunrise to sunset year-round.

Maps
No map is necessary for this short and easy walk.

Directions
From the junction of Routes 202 and 122 in New Salem, follow Route 202 south for 0.4 mile. Turn right onto Elm Street, drive 0.7 mile, and then turn left onto Neilson Road. Drive 0.5 mile and park at the roadside. The entrance is on the right, where a short trail leads to the gorge.

Contact
The Trustees of Reservations Central Region Office, Doyle Reservation, 325 Lindell Avenue, Leominster, MA 01453-5414, 978/840-4446, website: www.thetrustees.org.

4 MOUNT WATATIC AND NUTTING HILL
in Ashburnham

Total distance: 2.8 miles round-trip   **Hiking time:** 1.5 hours

Difficulty: 2   **Rating:** 9

Mount Watatic's 1,832-foot elevation barely qualifies it as anything but a big hill. But the pair of barren, rocky summits offer excellent views of nearby peaks such as Wachusett Mountain (see listings in this chapter) and New Hampshire's Monadnock, as well as the entire Wapack Range extending north and, on a clear day, landmarks as distant as Mount Greylock (see listings in The Berkshires and Western Massachusetts chapter), New Hampshire's White Mountains, and the Boston skyline. Watatic can feel like a bigger mountain, especially when the wind kicks up on its exposed crown. This loop encompasses Nutting Hill, where the flat, open summit offers some views. The Midstate Trail was rerouted in recent years to coincide with the Wapack Trail over Watatic's summit; both are well blazed with yellow triangles.

From the parking area, follow an old woods road north, ascending gradually. At 0.3 mile, the Wapack/Midstate Trail turns right (east), reaching the Watatic summit in another mile. Instead, this hike continues straight ahead on the blue-blazed State Line Trail (following the former route of the Midstate Trail). A half mile farther, you reach a junction where the State Line Trail forks left; continue straight ahead onto the Midstate Trail, which itself rejoins the Wapack Trail within another 0.2 mile. It is nearly a mile to Watatic's summit from this point. Turn right (southeast), soon passing over Nutting Hill's open top; watch for cairns leading directly over the hill and into the woods. Climbing Watatic's northwest slope, you pass somewhat overgrown trails of the former Mount Watatic ski area. Just below the summit stands an abandoned fire tower, now closed and unsafe. From the summit, an unmarked path leads to the lower, southeast summit. Double back to the fire tower, turn left, and follow the Wapack, passing an open ledge with views and, farther down, an enormous split boulder. At the Midstate Trail junction, turn left for the parking area.

User Groups

Hikers, snowshoers, and dogs. No wheelchair facilities. This trail is not suitable for bikes, horses, or skis. Hunting is allowed in season.

Access and Fees

Parking and access are free.

Maps

An excellent map of the Wapack Trail is available for $4 (including postage) from the Friends of the Wapack; the organization also sells a detailed guidebook to the entire trail for $11 (including postage). The *Guide to the Wapack Trail in Massachusetts & New Hampshire,* a three-color map, costs $3.95 from New England Cartographics, 413/549-4124 or toll-free 888/995-6277, website: www.necartographics.com. For a topographic area map, request Ashburnham from USGS Map Sales, Federal Center, Box 25286, Denver, CO 80225, 888/ASK-USGS (888/275-8747), website: http://mapping.usgs.gov.

Directions

The trailhead parking area is on the north side of Route 119 in Ashburnham, 1.4 miles west of its junction with Route 101.

Contact

Friends of the Wapack, P.O. Box 115, West Peterborough, NH 03468, website: www.wapack.org.

5 WILLARD BROOK
in Willard Brook State Forest in Ashby

Total distance: 2 miles round-trip   **Hiking time:** 1 hour

Difficulty: 1   **Rating:** 7

This easy walk hugs the rock-strewn Willard Brook through its tight valley, winding through hemlock groves and among huge boulders. This is a good, gentle hike for introducing very young children to the woods. The trail begins from either side of the stone bridge over Willard Brook, just below Damon Pond. Toward the other (northeast) end of the trail, it ascends a hillside and reaches a forest road; turning left brings you shortly to the state forest headquarters. Most people just double back to the start. There are several miles of woods roads in the state forest open to other activities, such as mountain biking or horseback riding.

User Groups
Hikers, dogs, skiers, and snowshoers. Dogs must be leashed. No wheelchair facilities. Bikes and horses are prohibited. Hunting is allowed in season.

Access and Fees
A daily parking fee of $5 is collected from mid-May to mid-October.

Maps
A free, basic trail map of the state forest is available at the headquarters on Route 119 in West Townsend, just before the Ashby town line, or at the Massachusetts Division of State Parks and Recreation website. For a topographic area map, request Ashburnham from USGS Map Sales, Federal Center, Box 25286, Denver, CO 80225, 888/ASK-USGS (888/275-8747), website: http://mapping.usgs.gov.

Directions
Park at the Damon Pond entrance off Route 119 in Ashby, 1.3 miles west of the Willard Brook State Forest headquarters and 0.2 mile east of the junction of Routes 119 and 31. The gate is closed in winter, so park in the roadside pullout.

Contact

Willard Brook State Forest, Route 119, West Townsend, MA 01474, 978/597-8802. Massachusetts Division of State Parks and Recreation, 251 Causeway Street, Suite 600, Boston, MA 02114-2104, 617/626-1250, website: www.state.ma.us/dem/forparks.htm.

6 CROW HILLS

in Leominster State Forest in Westminster

Total distance: 0.7 miles round-trip   **Hiking time:** 0.75 hour

Difficulty: 2   **Rating:** 9

The hike up Crow Hills, at the western edge of the more than 4,000-acre Leominster State Forest, is a short loop that can be done with young children, though it gets steep and rocky in brief sections (where you would have to remove snowshoes and watch for ice in winter). Despite its brevity and the climb of just a few hundred feet, it is one of the most dramatic walks in central Massachusetts, traversing the top of tall cliffs with commanding views of the wooded hills and ponds of the state forest and of Wachusett Mountain (see listings in this chapter).

From the parking lot, cross Route 31 to a wide, well-marked trail entering the woods. Within 100 feet, the trail turns sharply left, then swings right and climbs steeply to the base of cliffs, 100 feet high in places. The trail then diverges right and left, with both branches looping up to the clifftops. You can hike the loop in either direction; this description leads to the right (counter-

two of the author's nieces enjoying Crow Hills

clockwise). Walk below the cliff to where stones arranged in steps lead steeply uphill to a junction with the Midstate Trail, marked by yellow triangular blazes. Turn left, carefully following the trail atop the cliffs past several spots that offer sweeping views; the best views are at the far end of the cliffs. Wachusett Mountain, with its ski slopes, is visible to the southwest. Take care not to kick any loose stones or wander near the cliff's edge; there are often rock climbers and hikers below.

From the last open ledges, the Midstate Trail swings right, entering the woods again and continuing about 75 yards, then turning left and descending a steep, rocky gully. At its bottom, turn left again and, diverging from the Midstate, walk the trail around the base of the cliffs to this loop's beginning. Turn right and descend to the parking lot.

User Groups
Hikers, snowshoers, and dogs. Dogs must be leashed. No wheelchair facilities. This trail is not suitable for bikes, horses, or skis. Hunting is allowed in season.

Access and Fees
From May to October, a $5 parking fee is collected; a season pass costs $35. The parking lot may not always be plowed in winter; call the state forest headquarters for more information.

Maps
A free, basic trail map of Leominster State Forest is available at the state forest headquarters or at the Massachusetts Division of State Parks and Recreation website. The *Mount Wachusett and Leominster State Forest Trail Map* costs $3.95 from New England Cartographics, 413/549-4124 or toll-free 888/995-6277, website: www.necartographics.com. For a topographic area map, request Fitchburg from USGS Map Sales, Federal Center, Box 25286, Denver, CO 80225, 888/ASK-USGS (888/275-8747), website: http://mapping.usgs.gov.

Directions
The hike begins from a large parking lot at the Crow Hills Pond Picnic Area along Route 31 on the Westminster/Princeton line,

2.2 miles south of the junction of Routes 31 and 2, and 1.5 miles north of the junction of Routes 31 and 140.

Contact

Leominster State Forest, Route 31, Princeton, MA 01541, 978/874-2303. Massachusetts Division of State Parks and Recreation, 251 Causeway Street, Suite 600, Boston, MA 02114-2104, 617/626-1250, website: www.state.ma.us/dem/forparks.htm.

7 BALL HILL LOOP

in Leominster State Forest in Westminster, Princeton,
and Leominster

Total distance: 3.5 miles round-trip   **Hiking time:** 2.5 hours

Difficulty: 3   **Rating:** 7

Leominster State Forest has a network of marked trails and less-distinct footpaths weaving throughout, most in its northern half, north of Rocky Pond Road/Parmenter Road. (South of that dirt road, which is open to bikes but not motor vehicles, the state forest is crossed mainly by old woods roads.) This hike ascends one of the low, wooded hills in the state forest, into an area I've wandered into countless times—having grown up in Leominster—but where I still run across trails I don't recognize or end up someplace I did not expect to end up. There are myriad trails through here, and it's easy to get lost once you venture over Ball Hill. Nonetheless, it's a quiet woodlands that's fun to explore. This hike ascends small hills but never climbs more than a few hundred feet.

From the parking area, walk across the earthen dike between the two halves of Crow Hills Pond and then turn right, following a blazed trail south along the shore of the pond. Within 0.5 mile, turn left (east) onto the Rocky Pond Trail, which climbs Ball Hill, steeply for short stretches. Near the hilltop, about one mile from the hike's start, is a spot where the trees thin enough to allow a partially obstructed view of the hills to the west. Anyone concerned about getting lost might want to turn back from here. Otherwise, continue over the hill, through quiet woods crossed by the occasional stone wall.

Descending the back side of the hill, ignore the trails branching off to the right. Turn left at the first opportunity; about 2.5 miles from the parking area, you see a landfill through the trees at the state forest edge. The trail swings north, then west; continue bearing left at trail junctions. On your way back, you pass through a wet area, over a low hillock, and eventually reach the paved parking lot at the public beach at the Crow Hills Pond north end. Cross the parking lot to the south (left), picking up the trail again for the short walk back to the dike across the pond.

User Groups

Hikers, snowshoers, and dogs. Dogs must be leashed. No wheel-chair facilities. This trail is not suitable for bikes, horses, or skis. Hunting is allowed in season.

Access and Fees

From May to October, a $5 parking fee is collected; a season pass costs $35. The parking lot may not always be plowed in winter; call the state forest headquarters for more information.

Maps

A free, basic trail map of Leominster State Forest is available at the state forest headquarters or at the Massachusetts Division of State Parks and Recreation website. The *Mount Wachusett and Leominster State Forest Trail Map* costs $3.95 from New England Cartographics, 413/549-4124 or toll-free 888/995-6277, website: www.necartographics.com. For a topographic area map, request Fitchburg from USGS Map Sales, Federal Center, Box 25286, Denver, CO 80225, 888/ASK-USGS (888/275-8747), website: http://mapping.usgs.gov.

Directions

The hike begins from a large parking lot at the Crow Hills Pond Picnic Area along Route 31 on the Westminster-Princeton line, 2.2 miles south of the junction of Routes 31 and 2 and 1.5 miles north of the junction of Routes 31 and 140.

Contact

Leominster State Forest, Route 31, Princeton, MA 01541, 978/874-2303. Massachusetts Division of State Parks and Recreation, 251 Causeway Street, Suite 600, Boston, MA 02114-2104, 617/626-1250, website: www.state.ma.us/dem/forparks.htm.

8 LEOMINSTER FOREST ROADS LOOP
in Leominster State Forest in Westminster, Princeton,
and Leominster

Total distance: 5.5 miles round-trip   **Hiking time:** 3 hours

Difficulty: 6   **Rating:** 7

This loop of approximately 5.5 miles largely follows old forest roads through the southern half of Leominster State Forest, making it particularly fun on cross-country skis or a mountain bike. I've skied this loop and other roads in here many times; I especially enjoy coming to this state forest in winter. There are small hills along these roads—nothing that is difficult to hike, but which can make skiing or biking moderately difficult.

From the parking lot, cross the picnic area and the earthen dike dividing the two halves of Crow Hills Pond. Across the dike, turn right (south), following the trail along the pond and past it about 0.7 mile to the dirt Rocky Pond Road (which is not open to motor vehicles). Cross Rocky Pond Road onto Wolf Rock Road and continue about a half mile. Where the road forks, bear right and then watch for an unmarked footpath diverging left within 0.2 mile (if you reach the state forest boundary near private homes, you've gone too far). Follow that winding, narrow path through the woods—I've seen tracks of deer, rabbit, and other animals here in winter—less than a half mile to Wolf Rock Road and turn right. You descend a steep hill on the road, turn left onto Center Road, and follow it about 1.2 miles to Parmenter Road. Turn left (west), climbing a hill and crossing from Leominster into Princeton, where the road becomes Rocky Pond Road. From the road's high point, continue west for less than a mile to the junction of Rocky Pond Road, Wolf Rock Road, and the trail from Crow Hills Pond; turn right on the trail to return to this hike's start.

Special note: Short sections of this loop follow hiking trails that would be difficult on a bike. Cyclists might instead begin this loop from the dirt parking area and gate where Rocky Pond Road crosses Route 31, 0.6 mile south of the main parking area described in the directions below. Pedal east on Rocky Pond Road for about 0.4 mile and then turn right onto the wide Wolf

Rock Road. Where the road forks, 05 mile further, bear left, staying on Wolf Rock, which leads to Center Road and the continuation of this hike.

User Groups
Hikers, bikers, dogs, skiers, and snowshoers. Dogs must be leashed. No wheelchair facilities. Horses are prohibited. Hunting is allowed in season.

Access and Fees
From May to October, a $5 parking fee is collected; a season pass costs $35. The parking lot may not always be plowed in winter; call the state forest headquarters for more information.

Maps
A free, basic trail map of Leominster State Forest is available at the state forest headquarters or at the Massachusetts Division of State Parks and Recreation website. The *Mount Wachusett and Leominster State Forest Trail Map* costs $3.95 from New England Cartographics, 413/549-4124 or toll-free 888/995-6277, website: www.necartographics.com. For a topographic area map, request Fitchburg from USGS Map Sales, Federal Center, Box 25286, Denver, CO 80225, 888/ASK-USGS (888/275-8747), website: http://mapping.usgs.gov.

Directions
The hike begins from a large parking lot at the Crow Hills Pond Picnic Area along Route 31 on the Westminster/Princeton line, 2.2 miles south of the junction of Routes 31 and 2, and 1.5 miles north of the junction of Routes 31 and 140.

Contact
Leominster State Forest, Route 31, Princeton, MA 01541, 978/874-2303. Massachusetts Division of State Parks and Recreation, 251 Causeway Street, Suite 600, Boston, MA 02114-2104, 617/626-1250, website: www.state.ma.us/dem/forparks.htm.

9 MONOOSNOC RIDGE TRAIL

in Leominster

Total distance: 10.5 miles round-trip   **Hiking time:** 5 hours

Difficulty: 6   **Rating:** 7

My parents hiked this trail after it opened in 2000 and promptly
informed me that it belonged in this book. After a reconnais-
sance with them, I agreed. This pleasant hike of about 10.5 miles
across public land in my hometown came about thanks to the
Leominster Land Trust, with assistance from the Trustees of
Reservations Central Region Office, and the cooperation of the
city of Leominster. It traverses hilltops with some ups and downs
and occasional views, and makes for a great, quiet stroll in the
woods, a trail run, or winter outing on snowshoes. The Leominster Land Trust is working on developing a network of trails and
linking the Monoosnoc Ridge Trail and others with the trails of
nearby Leominster State Forest.

The Monoosnoc Ridge Trail is well marked with blue blazes and
signs at the trailheads and road crossings. It intersects other trails
and forest roads, so watch for the blazes. You can hike it end-to-
end from either endpoint trailhead, or hike a section of it by leaving a second vehicle at one of the road crossings. The Granite
Street, Elm Street, Wachusett Street, and Pleasant Street crossings
allow you to bite off pieces of the trail for outings of 1.5, three, six,
or nine miles.

User Groups

Hikers, bikers, snowshoers, and dogs. Parts of this trail would be
difficult to ski (probably requiring more than a foot of snow cov-
erage). No wheelchair facilities. Horses are prohibited. Hunting
is allowed in season.

Access and Fees

Parking and access are free.

Maps

A free trail map is available through the Leominster Land Trust,
Trustees of Reservations Central Region Office, and the Leominster

Recreation Department. The Leominster Land Trust also plans to place maps at the trailhead kiosks. For a topographic area map, request Fitchburg from USGS Map Sales, Federal Center, Box 25286, Denver, CO 80225, 888/ASK-USGS (888/275-8747), website: http://mapping.usgs.gov.

Directions
The trail's endpoints are at a turnout at the end of West Street (which begins in the center of Leominster), and at the Samosett School off Union Street, less than a mile east of Pleasant Street. The trail crosses three paved streets: The northbound trail crosses Elm Street about 0.1 mile west of the power lines crossing the street, and enters the woods southbound about 0.2 mile west of the power lines. The trail crosses Wachusett Street less than 0.1 mile west of a small reservoir. It crosses Pleasant Street at Sholan Farms (where there is parking for about a dozen vehicles), 0.25 mile beyond its junction with Union and Wachusett Streets in Leominster. It also crosses the dirt, upper portion of Granite Street (where there is parking for several vehicles), up the street from Leominster High School. For directions to these streets, see a road map of Leominster.

Contact
Leominster Land Trust, 14 Monument Square, Suite 300, Leominster, MA 01453, 978/537-7451. Trustees of Reservations Central Region Office, Doyle Reservation, 325 Lindell Avenue, Leominster, MA 01453-5414, 978/840-4446, website: www.the trustees.org. Leominster Recreation Department, 978/534-7529.

10 WACHUSETT MOUNTAIN: BALANCED ROCK

in Wachusett Mountain State Reservation in Princeton

Total distance: 0.6 miles round-trip **Hiking time:** 0.5 hour

Difficulty: 2 **Rating:** 7

Balanced Rock is a glacial-erratic boulder that well lives up to its name. Pick up the Midstate Trail's yellow triangular blazes from the parking lot, behind and to the right of the lodge. Here the trail is also known as the Balanced Rock Trail. Follow it, climbing gently, for 0.3 mile to Balanced Rock. To finish this hike, return the way you came. Hikers looking for a bit more of an outing can continue on the Midstate Trail to the Wachusett summit via the Semuhenna and Harrington Trails and then descend the Old Indian Trail back to the Midstate to return—a loop of several miles. Consult the map and inquire at the visitors center for specific distances.

User Groups

Hikers, snowshoers, and dogs. Dogs must be leashed. No wheelchair facilities. This trail is not suitable for skis. Bikes and horses are prohibited. Hunting is allowed in season.

Access and Fees

A daily parking fee of $2 is collected from mid-May to mid-October.

Maps

A free contour map of hiking trails is available at the visitors center or at the Massachusetts Division of State Parks and Recreation website. The *Northern Berkshires/Southwestern Massachusetts/ Wachusett Mountain* map costs $5.95 in paper from the Appalachian Mountain Club, 800/262-4455, website: www.outdoors.org. The *Mount Wachusett and Leominster State Forest Trail Map* is $3.95 from New England Cartographics, 413/549-4124 or toll-free 888/995-6277, website: www.necartographics.com. For topographic area maps, request Sterling and Fitchburg from USGS Map Sales, Federal Center, Box 25286, Denver, CO 80225, 888/ASK-USGS (888/275-8747), website: http://mapping.usgs.gov.

Directions

From Route 140, 2.2 miles south of the junction of Routes 140 and 2 in Westminster and 1.8 miles north of the junction of Routes 140 and 31, turn onto Mile Hill Road, following signs to the Wachusett Mountain Ski Area. Drive a mile, turn right into the ski area parking lot, and then cross to the rear of the lot, behind the lodge. The Wachusett Mountain State Reservation Visitor Center is farther up Mile Hill Road.

Contact

Wachusett Mountain State Reservation, Mountain Road, P.O. Box 248, Princeton, MA 01541, 978/464-2987. Massachusetts Division of State Parks and Recreation, 251 Causeway Street, Suite 600, Boston, MA 02114-2104, 617/626-1250, website: www.state.ma.us/dem/forparks.htm.

11 WACHUSETT MOUNTAIN: PINE HILL TRAIL

in Wachusett Mountain State Reservation in Princeton

Total distance: 2 miles round-trip   **Hiking time:** 1.5 hours

Difficulty: 4   **Rating:** 8

At 2,006 feet and the biggest hill in central Massachusetts, Wachusett may be better known for its downhill ski area. But the state reservation has a fairly extensive network of fine hiking trails, including a section of the Midstate Trail that passes over the summit. The summit offers views in all directions—on a clear day, you can see New Hampshire's Mount Monadnock to the north and the Boston skyline 40 miles to the east. Trail junctions are marked with signs. The Pine Hill Trail is a steep, rocky climb that could be dangerous in snowy or icy conditions.

From the visitors center parking lot, follow the Bicentennial Trail about 0.1 mile to the first trail branching off to the right, the Pine Hill Trail—actually an old ski trail and the most direct route to the summit, about a half mile. The trail ascends at a moderate grade over fairly rocky terrain. After checking out the views from various spots on the broad summit, cross to its southwest corner and look for the Harrington Trail sign. Descending the Harrington, you soon cross the paved summit road; after reentering the woods, take a short side path left off the Harrington to enjoy a long view west over the sparsely populated hills and valleys of central Massachusetts. Backtrack and descend the Harrington to the Link Trail, turning left. Turn right onto the Mountain House Trail, descend briefly, and then bear left onto the Loop Trail, which descends to the Bicentennial. Turn left for the visitors center.

User Groups

Hikers and dogs. Dogs must be leashed. No wheelchair facilities. This trail would be difficult to snowshoe or ski. Bikes and horses are prohibited. Hunting is allowed in season.

Access and Fees

A daily parking fee of $2 is collected from mid-May to mid-October.

Maps

A free contour map of hiking trails is available at the visitors center at the Massachusetts Division of State Parks and Recreation website. The *Northern Berkshires/Southwestern Massachusetts/Wachusett Mountain* map costs $5.95 in paper from the Appalachian Mountain Club, 800/262-4455, website: www.outdoors.org. The *Mount Wachusett and Leominster State Forest Trail Map* is $3.95 from New England Cartographics, 413/549-4124 or toll-free 888/995-6277, website: www.necartographics.com. For topographic area maps, request Sterling and Fitchburg from USGS Map Sales, Federal Center, Box 25286, Denver, CO 80225, 888/ASK-USGS (888/ 275-8747), website: http://mapping.usgs.gov.

Directions

From Route 140, 2.2 miles south of the junction of Routes 140 and 2 in Westminster and 1.8 miles north of the junction of Routes 140 and 31, turn onto Mile Hill Road, following signs to the Wachusett Mountain State Reservation Visitor Center.

Contact

Wachusett Mountain State Reservation, Mountain Road, P.O. Box 248, Princeton, MA 01541, 978/464-2987. Massachusetts Division of State Parks and Recreation, 251 Causeway Street, Suite 600, Boston, MA 02114-2104, 617/626-1250, website: www.state .ma.us/dem/forparks.htm.

12 WACHUSETT MOUNTAIN LOOP

in Wachusett Mountain State Reservation in Princeton

Total distance: 5 miles round-trip   **Hiking time:** 3 hours

Difficulty: 6   **Rating:** 8

See the trail notes for the Wachusett Mountain: Pine Hill Trail (previous listing) for more description about Wachusett Mountain. This hike takes a much more circuitous—and in many respects more enjoyable—route around the mountain than the previous hike, taking advantage of the extensive trail network here. Although sections of this route are somewhat rocky and steep for brief stretches, it's not very difficult, ascending about 700 feet in elevation. I've run it numerous times, and on parts of this loop you can escape the crowds that congregate at the summit and on the trails nearer to the visitors center. You can easily shorten or lengthen this hike as well; check out the trail map and improvise from this description. A scenic alternative is the Jack Frost Trail, which passes through dense hemlock forest.

From the visitors center parking lot, follow the Bicentennial Trail for about a mile as it contours around the mountain's base, passing three trail junctions, then bear left onto the High Meadow Trail. Follow it across an open meadow and then back into the woods again before reaching Echo Lake. Stay to the left on the gravel road beside the lake for about 0.1 mile, turn left on the Echo Lake Trail, and follow it less than a half mile to a parking lot. Crossing the small lot, pick up the Stage Coach Trail, climbing steadily up an old carriage road, which narrows to a footpath. After more than a half mile, bear right on the Harrington Trail. It crosses West Road, then the Administration Road, before suddenly growing much steeper as it makes a direct line for the summit. But right before that steep part begins, turn left on the Semuhenna Trail, staying on it for about a half mile. Cross the paved summit road, reenter the woods, and then immediately turn right on the West Side Trail. You're on that path for less than a half mile before turning right again on the Old Indian Trail, the steepest part of this hike, as you climb to the summit, passing a ski area chairlift station right before reaching the top. Cross the summit to the paved road that heads down, follow it about 100 feet, and then bear right into the woods on the Mountain House Trail. Descend about a quarter mile, turn left, continue another quarter mile or less, and turn left again on the Loop Trail, descending over rocks to the Bicentennial Trail. Turn left for the visitors center.

User Groups
Hikers, snowshoers, and dogs. Dogs must be leashed. No wheelchair facilities. This trail is not suitable for skis. Bikes and horses are prohibited. Hunting is allowed in season.

Access and Fees
A daily parking fee of $2 is collected from mid-May to mid-October.

Maps
A free contour map of hiking trails is available at the visitors center or at the Massachusetts Division of State Parks and Recreation website. The *Northern Berkshires/Southwestern Massachusetts/ Wachusett Mountain* map costs $5.95 in paper from the Appalachian Mountain Club, 800/262-4455, website: www.outdoors.org. The *Mount Wachusett and Leominster State Forest Trail Map* is $3.95 from New England Cartographics, 413/549-4124 or toll-free 888/995-6277, website: www.necartographics.com. For topographic area maps, request Sterling and Fitchburg from USGS Map Sales, Federal Center, Box 25286, Denver, CO 80225, 888/ASK-USGS (888/275-8747), website: http://mapping.usgs.gov.

Directions
From Route 140, 2.2 miles south of the junction of Routes 140 and 2 in Westminster and 1.8 miles north of the junction of Routes 140 and 31, turn onto Mile Hill Road, following signs to the Wachusett Mountain State Reservation Visitor Center.

Contact
Wachusett Mountain State Reservation, Mountain Road, P.O. Box 248, Princeton, MA 01541, 978/464-2987. Massachusetts Division of State Parks and Recreation, 251 Causeway Street, Suite 600, Boston, MA 02114-2104, 617/626-1250, website: www.state .ma.us/dem/forparks.htm.

13 REDEMPTION ROCK TO WACHUSETT MOUNTAIN
in Princeton

Total distance: 1.8 miles round-trip   **Hiking time:** 1 hour

Difficulty: 2   **Rating:** 7

When I was a young boy, an uncle and aunt took my brothers, a sister, and me to Redemption Rock, a massive, flat-topped granite boulder just off the roadside. We climbed around on it, thinking we were on some great adventure—which, of course, we were. Years later, I took my young nephew and niece to Redemption Rock and let them have their own little adventure. Legend has it that a Concord settler named John Hoar sat atop this boulder with members of a band of King Phillip's Indians in 1676 to negotiate the release of Mary Rowlandson, wife of the minister in the nearby town of Lancaster, whom the Indians abducted and held captive for 11 weeks.

Redemption Rock is a fun spot for young children, and the walk through the woods to the base of Wachusett Mountain and back follows a fairly quiet Midstate Trail stretch where you might see a deer or grouse. After exploring Redemption Rock, which sits beside the parking area, follow the Midstate Trail's yellow triangular blazes into the woods. Watch closely for the blazes; several side trails branch off the Midstate. It proceeds generally westward through the woods, climbing slightly and traversing some rocky trail stretches and some wet areas, reaching Mountain Road and the parking lot for the Wachusett Mountain Ski Area in 0.9 mile. Turn around and return the way you came, or combine this with the Wachusett Mountain: Balanced Rock hike, which begins across the ski area parking lot.

User Groups
Hikers, snowshoers, and dogs. No wheelchair facilities. The trail is not suitable for bikes, horses, or skis. Hunting is allowed in season on the Midstate Trail, but is prohibited at Redemption Rock, which is a 0.25-mile preserve owned by The Trustees of Reservations.

Access and Fees

Parking and access are free. Redemption Rock is open to the public from sunrise to sunset year-round.

Maps

The *Mount Wachusett and Leominster State Forest Trail Map* is $3.95 from New England Cartographics, 413/549-4124 or toll-free 888/995-6277, website: www.necartographics.com. For topographic area maps, request Fitchburg and Sterling from USGS Map Sales, Federal Center, Box 25286, Denver, CO 80225, 888/ASK-USGS (888/275-8747), website: http://mapping.usgs.gov.

Directions

The hike begins from the small parking lot at Redemption Rock along Route 140 in Princeton, 3.1 miles south of the junction of Routes 140 and 2 in Westminster and 0.9 mile north of the junction of Routes 140 and 31 in Princeton.

Contact

The Trustees of Reservations Central Region Office, Doyle Reservation, 325 Lindell Avenue, Leominster, MA 01453-5414, 978/840-4446, website: www.thetrustees.org.

14 WACHUSETT MEADOW TO WACHUSETT MOUNTAIN

in Princeton

Total distance: 6.2 miles round-trip   **Hiking time:** 3.5 hours

Difficulty: 6   **Rating:** 8

Much of this Midstate Trail stretch is relatively easy, ascending less than 1,000 feet in elevation, much of that over the steep final 0.3-mile climb to the Wachusett Mountain summit, where there are long views in every direction. Visitors to Wachusett Meadow, a 977-acre nature preserve, might want to check out the loop of about 1.5 miles over Brown Hill, where the open crown affords 360-degree views. You also shouldn't miss the 300-year-old Crocker maple, one of the largest sugar maples in the country, with a trunk circumference of more than 15 feet. It sits on the west edge of the meadow, a very short detour off this hike's route, and it is guaranteed to awe children.

From the parking area, walk north into the meadow on the Mountain Trail and then turn left in the middle of the meadow at post six, heading for the woods and reaching a junction with the Midstate Trail about 0.2 mile from the parking lot. Turn right (north), following the Midstate over easy terrain through the woods. The trail crosses a dirt road about a mile from the hike's start, passes over a small hill, and then crosses paved Westminster Road at 1.8 miles. After crossing a field, the trail enters the woods again, ascending a low hill and passing just below the summit. (You can bushwhack a short distance off trail to the hilltop and see a wind farm of windmills, then double back to the trail.) After crossing paved Administration Road, the Midstate Trail—here also called the Harrington Trail—reaches a junction with the Semuhenna Trail one mile from Westminster Road. The Semuhenna/Midstate turns left, but this hike continues straight up the Harrington another 0.3 mile to the Wachusett Mountain summit. Hike back the way you came.

Special note: To avoid backtracking, and for a somewhat shorter hike, shuttle vehicles to Wachusett Meadow and the Wachusett Mountain State Reservation Visitor Center and do this hike one-way; then descend the Pine Hill Trail and Bicentennial Trail to the Wachusett Mountain Visitor Center, as described in the Redemption Rock to Wachusett Mountain hike.

User Groups
Hikers and snowshoers. No wheelchair facilities. This trail is not suitable for horses. Bikes, dogs, hunting, and skis are prohibited.

Access and Fees
A fee of $4 per adult and $3 per child age 3–12 and seniors is charged at Wachusett Meadow to nonmembers of the Massachusetts Audubon Society. The Wachusett Meadow Visitor Center trails are open dawn to dusk, Tuesday–Sunday and on Monday holidays. The Nature Center is open Tuesday–Saturday, 10 A.M.– 2 P.M. A daily parking fee of $2 is collected from mid-May to mid-October at Wachusett Mountain State Reservation.

Maps
A map of Wachusett Meadow is available at an information board beside the parking lot. A free contour map of hiking trails in the Wachusett Mountain State Reservation is available at the state reservation or at the Massachusetts Division of State Parks and Recreation website. The *Northern Berkshires/Southwestern Massachusetts/Wachusett Mountain* map costs $5.95 in paper from the Appalachian Mountain Club, 800/262-4455, website: www.outdoors.org. The *Mount Wachusett and Leominster State Forest Trail Map* is $3.95 from New England Cartographics, 413/549-4124 or toll-free 888/995-6277, website: www.necartographics.com. For a topographic area map, request Sterling from USGS Map Sales, Federal Center, Box 25286, Denver, CO 80225, 888/ASK-USGS (888/275-8747), website: http://mapping.usgs.gov.

Directions
From the junction of Routes 62 and 31 in Princeton center, drive west on Route 62 for 0.5 mile and turn right onto Goodnow Road at a sign for the Wachusett Meadow Sanctuary. Continue a mile to the end of the paved road and park at the sanctuary visitors center.

Contact
Massachusetts Audubon Society Wachusett Meadow Wildlife

Sanctuary, 113 Goodnow Road, Princeton, MA 01541, 978/464-2712, email: wachusett@massaudubon.org. Massachusetts Audubon Society, 208 South Great Road, Lincoln, MA 01773, 781/259-9500 or 800/AUDUBON, website: www.massaudubon.org. Wachusett Mountain State Reservation, Mountain Road, P.O. Box 248, Princeton, MA 01541, 978/464-2987. Massachusetts Division of State Parks and Recreation, 251 Causeway Street, Suite 600, Boston, MA 02114-2104, 617/626-1250, website: www.state.ma.us/dem/forparks.htm.

15 MOUNT HOLYOKE
in Skinner State Park in Hadley

Total distance: 3.2 miles round-trip **Hiking time:** 2 hours

Difficulty: 3 **Rating:** 8

Along the up-and-down ridge of 878-foot Mount Holyoke, the Summit House stands out prominently, easily visible to I-91 motorists several miles to the west. Although mostly wooded, this rugged ridgeline has several overlooks that afford splendid views west to the Connecticut Valley and the Berkshires, and some views southward. This hike climbs about 700 feet in elevation.

Follow the Metacomet-Monadnock Trail east from the road, immediately climbing a steep hillside; the trail soon swings north and ascends the ridge, reaching the first views in just over 0.5 mile. At 1.6 miles, the trail passes by the historic Summit House, once a fashionable mountaintop hotel and now part of the state park; it's open weekends from Memorial Day to Columbus Day for tours and programs; there are picnic grounds. The Connecticut Valley views from here are excellent. You can return the way you came or continue over the summit, crossing the paved Mountain Road and turning right (south) in Taylor's Notch onto the red-blazed Dry Brook Trail. Follow it down the small valley, trending to the southwest and finally to the west and back to your vehicle.

User Groups
Hikers, snowshoers, and dogs. Dogs must be leashed. No wheelchair facilities. This trail is not suitable for bikes, horses, or skis. Hunting is prohibited.

Access and Fees
Parking and access are free.

Maps
A free trail map of Skinner State Park is available at the Halfway House on Mountain Road (off Route 47) when a staff person is there; at the Notch Visitor Center on Route 116, where the Metacomet-Monadnock Trail crosses the road and enters Holyoke

Range State Park in Amherst; or at the Massachusetts Division of State Parks and Recreation website. The *Blue Hills Reservation/ Mount Tom/Holyoke Range* map costs $5.95 in paper from the Appalachian Mountain Club, 800/262-4455, website: www.outdoors.org. The *Holyoke Range/Skinner State Park Trail Map (Western Section)* costs $3.95 from New England Cartographics, 413/549-4124 or toll-free 888/995-6277, website:www.necartographics.com. For a topographic area map, request Mount Holyoke from USGS Map Sales, Federal Center, Box 25286, Denver, CO 80225, 888/ ASK-USGS (888/275-8747), website: http://mapping.usgs.gov.

Directions
From the junction of Routes 47 and 9 in Hadley, drive south on Route 47 for 4.9 miles (you'll see the Summit House on the Mount Holyoke ridge straight ahead). Across from the Hockanum Cemetery, turn left, continue 0.1 mile, and park at the roadside where the white blazes of the Metacomet-Monadnock Trail enter the woods on the right. Or from the junction of Routes 47 and 116 in South Hadley, drive north on Route 47 for 2.7 miles, turn right at Hockanum Cemetery, and then continue 0.1 mile to the trailhead.

Contact
Skinner State Park, Route 47, Box 91, Hadley, MA 01035, 413/586-0350 or 413/253-2883. Massachusetts Division of State Parks and Recreation, 251 Causeway Street, Suite 600, Boston, MA 02114-2104, 617/626-1250, website: www.state.ma.us/dem/forparks.htm.

16 PURGATORY CHASM

in Purgatory Chasm State Reservation in Sutton

Total distance: 0.5 miles round-trip   **Hiking time:** 0.5 hour

Difficulty: 1   **Rating:** 8

On this adventure, you scramble over rocks into the mouth of a chasm stretching 0.25 mile before you, its floor littered with huge boulders. The air is often at least 10 degrees cooler than in the parking lot you've just left behind. Rock walls rise as high at 70 feet on either side of this narrow defile, which geologists theorize was created by catastrophic force after melting glacial ice suddenly released torrents of flood water that shattered this gap through the granite bedrock. As if clinging to its prehistoric roots, Purgatory Chasm today is known to harbor pockets of ice into May and June. Although the scrambling can be difficult for people who are uncomfortable moving over rocks, this 0.5-mile loop is mostly flat and a good one for children.

From the information kiosk, walk toward the pavilion, but before reaching it turn right where the blue-blazed Chasm Loop Trail leads down through the chasm; you may see rock climbers on the walls. At the chasm's far end, poke your head inside the aptly named Coffin, a tight space among the boulders to the trail's right. Then turn left and follow the Chasm Loop Trail's blue blazes uphill onto the rim above the chasm, past deep cracks that have been given such names as Fat Man's Misery and the Corn Crib. The trail leads back to the parking lot.

User Groups

Hikers and dogs. Dogs must be leashed. No wheelchair facilities. The trail may be difficult to snowshoe, depending on snow conditions, and is not suitable for bikes, horses, or skis. Hunting is allowed in season.

Access and Fees

Parking and access are free. Purgatory Chasm State Reservation is open sunrise to sunset daily, year-round.

Maps

A free map of hiking trails is available at the information kiosk and at the Massachusetts Division of State Parks and Recreation website. For topographic area maps, request Milford and Worcester South from USGS Map Sales, Federal Center, Box 25286, Denver, CO 80225, 888/ASK-USGS (888/275-8747), website: http://mapping.usgs.gov.

Directions

From Route 146 in Northbridge, take the exit for Purgatory Road. Turn west on Purgatory Road and drive 0.6 mile to parking on the left, beside a pavilion and information kiosk.

Contact

Purgatory Chasm State Reservation, Purgatory Road, Sutton, MA 01590, 508/234-3733. Massachusetts Division of State Parks and Recreation, 251 Causeway Street, Suite 600, Boston, MA 02114-2104, 617/626-1250, website: www.state.ma.us/dem/forparks.htm.

17 MIDSTATE TRAIL LOOP
in Douglas State Forest in Douglas

Total distance: 6.5 miles round-trip   **Hiking time:** 3.5 hours

Difficulty: 6   **Rating:** 7

This loop, mostly on forest roads, uses the Midstate Trail to explore the big piece of Douglas State Forest that lies south of Route 16. The state forest also extends north of Route 16 and is worth exploring further. The loop sections that employ forest roads are easy or moderately difficult for mountain bikers; however, the stretches that follow a rougher trail are more difficult. The Midstate is fairly flat but crosses some streams and gets rocky in places. It's a well-blazed trail with yellow triangles, yet most other forest roads are not marked; use the map.

The Midstate Trail is accessed via the Coffeehouse Loop's southern arm, a forest road beginning at the south end of the parking lot. When you reach the Midstate, turn right (north) onto it. The Midstate makes several turns and, three miles out, reaches a T intersection at a forest road; you'll probably hear traffic on Route 16 to the left. This loop turns right, following the forest road south. At a fork, bear right and cross the dirt Southwest Main Street (where, if you turned left, you would shortly reach the intersection of Cedar Road and Wallum Street). The next intersection reconnects you with the Midstate Trail; backtrack on the Midstate southbound to return.

User Groups
Hikers, bikers, dogs, horses, skiers, and snowshoers. Dogs must be leashed. No wheelchair facilities. Hunting is allowed in season.

Access and Fees
A daily parking fee of $5 is collected from mid-May to mid-October. The fee can be avoided by accessing the state forest at other roadside parking areas. Consult the map for other access points.

Maps
A free trail map and informational brochure are available at the park entrance or at the Massachusetts Division of State Parks

and Recreation website. For a topographic area map, request Webster from USGS Map Sales, Federal Center, Box 25286, Denver, CO 80225, 888/ASK-USGS (888/275-8747), website: http://mapping.usgs.gov.

Directions

From I-395, take Exit 2 for Route 16 east. Drive 5.1 miles and turn right onto Cedar Road (there may be no street sign) at the sign for Douglas State Forest. Drive 1.8 miles to a crossroads at Southwest Main Street and proceed straight through onto Wallum Street. At 0.9 mile farther, turn right into the state forest and drive 0.7 mile to an information panel where a box contains maps. Bear right and continue a short distance to a parking lot.

Contact

Douglas State Forest, 107 Wallum Lake Road, Douglas, MA 01516, 508/476-7872. Massachusetts Division of State Parks and Recreation, 251 Causeway Street, Suite 600, Boston, MA 02114-2104, 617/626-1250, website: www.state.ma.us/dem/forparks.htm.

18 COFFEEHOUSE LOOP

in Douglas State Forest in Douglas

Total distance: 2.2 miles round-trip   **Hiking time:** 1.5 hours

Difficulty: 1   **Rating:** 7

This relatively flat trail makes an easy loop through peaceful woods, with the terrain growing slightly rocky in some places. Easy to follow, with trail junctions clearly signed, this hike also offers access to a longer outing on the Midstate Trail for those with extra time and energy. The loop begins at the parking lot's north end, eventually reaches and coincides for a short distance with the Midstate Trail southbound, then diverges left from the Midstate Trail and returns to the parking lot via a forest road.

User Groups

Hikers, dogs, skiers, and snowshoers. Dogs must be leashed. No wheelchair facilities. Bikes and horses are prohibited on part of this loop. Hunting is allowed in season.

Access and Fees

A daily parking fee of $5 is collected from mid-May to mid-October. The fee can be avoided by accessing the state forest at other roadside parking areas. Consult the map for other access points.

Maps

A free trail map and informational brochure are available at the park entrance or at the Massachusetts Division of State Parks and Recreation website. For a topographic area map, request Webster from USGS Map Sales, Federal Center, Box 25286, Denver, CO 80225, 888/ASK-USGS (888/275-8747), website: http://mapping.usgs.gov.

Directions

From I-395, take Exit 2 for Route 16 east. Drive 5.1 miles and turn right onto Cedar Road (there may be no street sign) at the sign for Douglas State Forest. Drive 1.8 miles to a crossroads at Southwest Main Street and proceed straight through onto Wallum Street. At 0.9 mile farther, turn right into the state forest and drive 0.7 mile to an information panel where a box contains maps. Bear right and continue a short distance to a parking lot.

Contact

Douglas State Forest, 107 Wallum Lake Road, Douglas, MA 01516, 508/476-7872. Massachusetts Division of State Parks and Recreation, 251 Causeway Street, Suite 600, Boston, MA 02114-2104, 617/626-1250, website: www.state.ma.us/dem/forparks.htm.

Chapter 3

© MICHAEL LANZA

Greater Boston and Cape Cod

Greater Boston and Cape Cod

The Greater Boston area has a tremendous variety of hiking. The rocky and scenic Blue Hills and Middlesex Fells are oases of quiet, wooded hills amid metropolitan Boston, making them rare and cherished recreation areas. The unique coastal trails of the Cape Cod National Seashore put hikers in unusual microenvironments. Premier state lands like Bradley Palmer State Park and Myles Standish State Forest are sprawling, four-season recreation centers for thousands of local residents.

Likewise, the Trustees of Reservations properties—Noanet Woodlands, Rocky Woods, and World's End—provide valuable local places to walk, exercise, and sightsee. Maudslay State Park and Walden Pond State Park Reservation not only are great places to walk, but preserve invaluable pieces of local history. Great Meadows, Plum Island, and Caratunk are on the must-see destinations list of many bird-watchers. And to keep things interesting, this chapter even tosses in a few paved recreation paths.

Winter weather is erratic but generally milder in this area than much of New England, opening up opportunities for visiting many of these places year-round without having to deal with snow or extreme cold. More commonly, visitors must deal with wind and, in certain seasons, biting insects and traffic. Do a little research before you go. Regulations vary widely under these different land-management agencies; be aware of and respect them always.

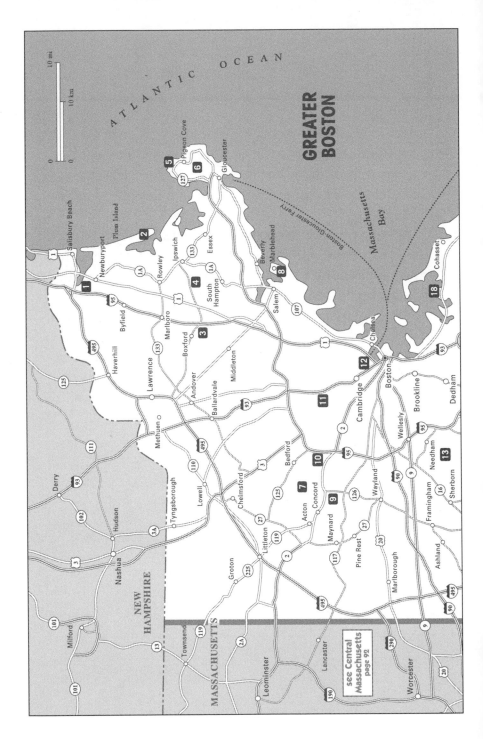

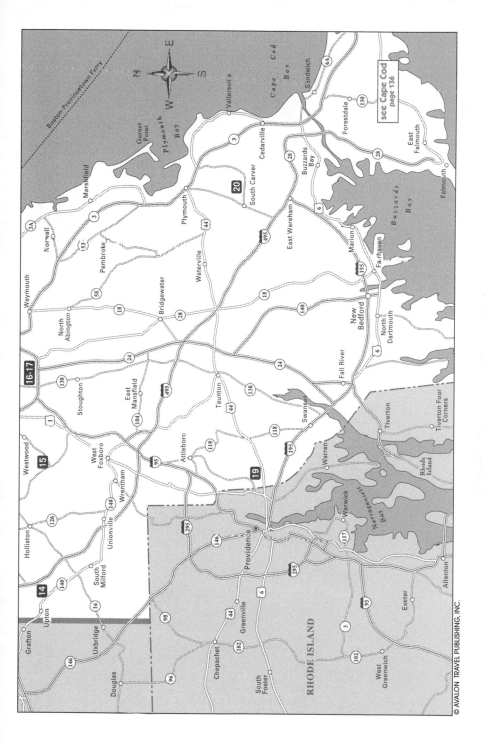

see Cape Cod
page 136

Boston-Provincetown Ferry

Cape Cod Bay

N
E
W
S

Sandwich

Vallersville

Plymouth Bay

Gurnet Point

130

Forestdale

East Falmouth

Marshfield

Cedarville

South Carver

Buzzards Bay

28

28

Falmouth

3

20

3A

Norwell

53

Pembroke

Plymouth

144

East Wareham

6

Buzzards Bay

Weymouth

58

Waterville

495

Marion

195

Fairhaven

North Abington

18

Bridgewater

28

18

140

New Bedford

North Dartmouth

6

16-17

138

Stoughton

24

East Mansfield

495

Taunton

138

24

Fall River

6

1

104

44

118

Swansea

195

Tiverton

Tiverton Four Corners

Westwood

15

West Foxboro

Attleboro

118

118

Warren

Rhode Island

126

140

Wrentham

95

19

Holliston

Unionville

295

146

Providence

Warwick

117

Narragansett Bay

14

140

South Milford

16

295

6

117

Grafton

Upton

Uxbridge

98

44

Greenville

3

Exeter

95

Allenton

146

Douglas

96

Chepachet

102

South Foster

RHODE ISLAND

West Greenwich

102

© AVALON TRAVEL PUBLISHING, INC.

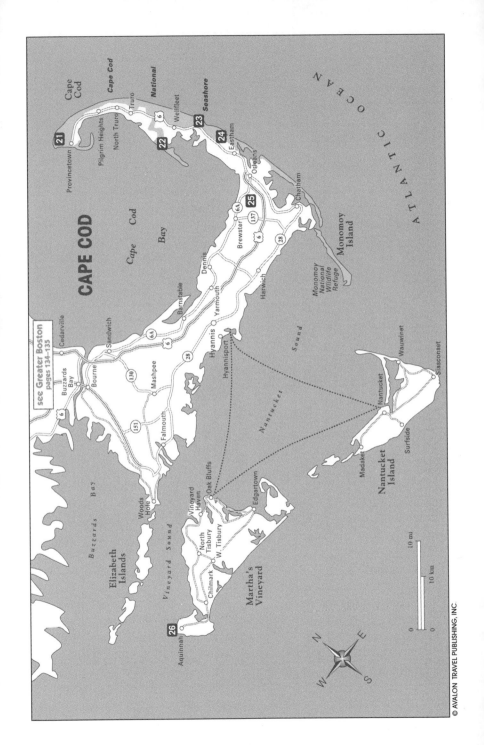

Contents

1 MAUDSLAY STATE PARK

in Newburyport

Total distance: 2.5 miles round-trip **Hiking time:** 1.5 hours

Difficulty: 1 **Rating:** 8

This 480-acre park on the Merrimack River was the 19th-century estate of the Moseleys, one of New England's wealthiest families. George Washington visited this area in 1789, and a regular ferry crossed the river here in the 17th century. Today you can hike trails through its many gardens and one of the largest naturally occurring mountain laurel stands in eastern Massachusetts, and stroll grounds where more flowers and plants bloom than I could begin to list. Mid-June is the time to catch the brilliant white flowers of the mountain laurel. The park sponsors numerous educational and recreational events. This hike is relatively flat.

From the parking lot, walk past the headquarters and turn right at a green gate onto Hedge Drive, a dirt road lined with trees and hedges. Near a small building, turn left and follow that road a short distance to its intersection with another road. You are across from the vegetable garden. Turn left, walk past buildings, and enter the Italian Garden. Walk straight through it onto a path that passes an old well, cross the dirt Main Road, and walk through a courtyard to the Merrimack River Trail, which is marked by blue, white, and green blazes. Straight ahead is the Merrimack River. Turn right onto the Merrimack River Trail, following it along the hilltop and down into woods. After crossing two brooks on wooden bridges, the trail bears left onto another road and crosses over a dam at the end of the Flowering Pond. Here you reach the Laurel Walk, where the Merrimack River Trail branches right and left. The area to the left is closed from November 1 to March 31; take the right branch during these months. Otherwise, turn left and follow the Merrimack River Trail along the riverbank. When it meets the Castle Hill Trail (and the Merrimack River Trail's other branch), turn left and stay with the Merrimack River Trail until you reach the end of a tree-lined road on your right; the Castle Hill Trail follows it up onto Castle Hill, where there are views of the state park and this corner of the Merrimack Valley. Over the hilltop, turn right onto one road, quickly left ònto another, and then right onto Line Road. It leads straight onto the Main Road (backtracking over the Merrimack River Trail's right branch). Take the stone bridge over the Flowering Pond, turn left onto the Pasture Trail, and follow it back to the parking lot.

User Groups
Hikers, bikers, dogs, horses, skiers, and snowshoers. Dogs must be leashed. No wheelchair facilities. Hunting is prohibited.

Access and Fees
A daily parking fee of $2 is collected year-round. The park is open 8 A.M.–sunset. Picnickers are welcome. A special-use permit is required for weddings, family reunions, and school groups.

Maps
A free, good trail map, including historical information and the seasons for viewing various park flora in bloom, is available at park headquarters. A basic map is also available at the Massachusetts Division of State Parks and Recreation website. For a topographic area map, request Newburyport from USGS Map Sales, Federal Center, Box 25286, Denver, CO 80225, 888/ASK-USGS (888/275-8747), website: http://mapping.usgs.gov.

Directions
From I-95, take Exit 57 in Newburyport for Route 113 west. Drive 0.5 mile and then turn right onto Hoyt's Lane/Gypsy Lane. At the road's end, turn right (in front of the park headquarters) onto Pine Hill Road and right again into the parking lot.

Contact
Maudslay State Park, Curzon's Mill Road, Newburyport, MA 01950, 978/465-7223. Massachusetts Division of State Parks and Recreation, 251 Causeway Street, Suite 600, Boston, MA 02114-2104, 617/626-1250, website: www.state.ma.us/dem/forparks.htm.

2 BAR HEAD DRUMLIN/PLUM ISLAND
in Sandy Point State Reservation in Ipswich

Total distance: 3 miles round-trip   **Hiking time:** 1.5 hours

Difficulty: 2   **Rating:** 7

This easy hike combines a walk along a sandy beach and a rocky shoreline with a hike onto the glacial drumlin, an oval mound of earth deposited by a receding glacier 10,000 years ago. Today several plant and animal species rarely found near a sandy beach thrive on Bar Head Drumlin. Fifty feet high and covering 15 acres, the drumlin is shrinking under constant erosion by the ocean. Nearby, the sprawling Parker River National Wildlife Refuge is home to numerous bird species in summer, including cormorants, herons, kingfishers, and ducks. The refuge also offers hiking opportunities. Nearly across from the parking area is an observation tower with a view of the refuge's marshlands. Bring bug repellent in summer—there are lots of biting insects, especially on the overgrown road along the refuge boundary. Inspect your skin and clothing afterward for ticks.

From the parking lot, pass through a gate onto the beach and turn right for the drumlin. Below the eroded cliffs of Bar Head, you walk a rock-strewn beach. Beyond the drumlin, the beach again becomes sandy. Follow the waterline around to the right until you reach a fence at the wildlife refuge boundary. Turn right and follow an overgrown road along the refuge boundary to a parking lot for the state reservation. Cross the lot to an unmarked, overgrown trail leading up onto Bar Head. Although the trees and brush atop the drumlin are too dense and high to afford views, a few side trails to the cliffs permit beach and ocean views. The trail leads over Bar Head and back to the beach near the boardwalk where you started.

User Groups
Hikers and snowshoers. No wheelchair facilities. This trail rarely receives enough snow for skis or snowshoes and is not suitable for horses. Bicycles are permitted only on the refuge road and in designated parking areas. Dogs are prohibited. Waterfowl hunting is permitted during fall and winter in designated salt marsh areas, and in fall, there is a controlled deer hunt on the island area of the refuge, with hunters chosen by lottery.

Access and Fees

Open daily sunrise–sunset. Walk only on trails, boardwalks, roads, parking areas, observation areas, and the beach; all other areas, including the dunes, are closed to the public. The beach is closed April 1 through at least July 1, portions possibly through late August, to protect nesting areas for the threatened piping plover. The fee for entering the Parker River National Wildlife Refuge is $5 per vehicle or $2 for anyone entering on foot or bike, year-round. During the warmer months, the refuge often fills to capacity and the entrance closes temporarily, even to visitors on foot. Arrive early to avoid this inconvenience.

Maps

No map is really needed for this hike, but two different maps are available at the refuge's website. For topographic area maps, request Ipswich and Newburyport from USGS Map Sales, Federal Center, Box 25286, Denver, CO 80225, 888/ASK-USGS (888/ 275-8747), website: http://mapping.usgs.gov.

Directions

From Route 95 take exit 57 and travel east on Route 113, then continue straight onto Route 1A South to the intersection with Rolfe's Lane for a total of 3.5 miles. Turn left onto Rolfe's Lane and travel 0.5 mile to its end. Turn right onto the Plum Island Turnpike and travel 2.0 miles crossing the Sgt. Donald Wilkinson Bridge to Plum Island. Take your first right onto Sunset Drive and travel 0.5 mile to the refuge entrance. From the entrance, drive 6.5 miles to a dirt lot at the end of the road and park.

Contact

Parker River National Wildlife Refuge, 6 Plum Island Turnpike, Newburyport, MA 01950, 978/465-5753 or 800/877-8339 for the hearing impaired, website: http://parkerriver.fws.gov/. Refuge headquarters is located at the north end of Plum Island near the Newburyport Harbor Lighthouse and is open Monday–Friday, 8 A.M.–4:30 P.M., except on federal holidays. U.S. Fish and Wildlife Service, 800/344-WILD, website: www.fws.gov.

③ BALD HILL

in Boxford State Forest

Total distance: 3 miles round-trip

Hiking time: 2 hours

Difficulty: 3

Rating: 7

Here is yet another sizable chunk of state land on the North Shore with a wealth of trails ideal for many activities. This loop takes you through the forest's southeast corner and over Bald Hill, but there's a lot more to this place worth checking out. You may stumble across old gravestones or home foundations from when this was farmland. This loop largely follows forest roads, is hilly, and the terrain can be rocky and rugged—a challenge on a mountain bike. Many trail intersections have numbered markers that correspond to numbers on the trail map. The forest tends toward the soggy, meaning a plague of mosquitoes in spring and early summer. This is a primo mountain biking destination during summer and fall, but avoid digging up the trails with bikes in mud season.

From the turnout, head past the gate onto the dirt Bald Hill Road. Past Crooked Pond, bear left at Intersection 14, and left again at Intersection 13. Farther along, turn right, climbing fairly steeply up Bald Hill. On its open summit, cross the field to the left and pick up a forest road heading back down. Bear right and you'll pass a stone foundation at the former Russell-Hooper farmhouse site (marked by a small sign). Just beyond it, to the right of the trail, is the Russell-Hooper barn site. Follow the trail around to the right. At Intersection 8A, turn right; eventually you follow white blazes. At Intersection 26, turn right again and follow this trail back to Intersection 13.

User Groups

Hikers, bikers, dogs, horses, skiers, and snowshoers. Dogs must be leashed. No wheelchair facilities. Hunting is allowed in season.

Access and Fees

Parking and access are free.

Maps

A trail map is available at the Massachusetts Division of State Parks and Recreation website.

Directions

From I-95 in Boxford, take Exit 51 for Endicott Road. Drive west and turn right onto Middleton Road. After passing Fuller Lane on the right, continue on Middleton Road another 0.8 mile. Park at a roadside turnout on the left.

Contact

Boxford State Forest, c/o Harold Parker State Forest, 1951 Turnpike Road, North Andover, MA 01845-6326, 978/686-3391. Massachusetts Division of State Parks and Recreation, 251 Causeway Street, Suite 600, Boston, MA 02114-2104, 617/626-1250, website: www.state.ma.us/dem/forparks.htm.

4 BRADLEY PALMER STATE PARK

in Topsfield

Total distance: 2.5 miles round-trip   **Hiking time:** 1.5 hours

Difficulty: 2   **Rating:** 7

Bradley Palmer was a famous attorney in the early 1900s who represented Sinclair Oil in the Teapot Dome Scandal and President Wilson at the Versailles Peace Conference after World War I. This park, named for Palmer, is a great multiuse recreational area. I lived on the North Shore a number of years ago, and this park was my favorite local place to cross-country ski. Its moderately sloping hills, wide forest roads, and rugged trails also offer very interesting and varied mountain biking and hiking. And the wildlife here might surprise you: Two friends of mine were mountain biking here when an owl with a squirrel in its talons swept just over their heads. This hike merely introduces you to this park; explore it further on your own.

From the parking area, cross the paved road and head onto a broad forest road. Bear left and start climbing Blueberry Hill (a rigorous climb on a bike). Take the third right onto another forest road and then the second left to reach the open hilltop. If you imagine entering the hilltop meadow at six o'clock, cross the hilltop and turn right, toward a road entering the woods at about three o'clock. Watch for a narrower trail exiting left off that road and follow it down a steep hill. Bear right onto another trail, which leads down to the Ipswich River and land in the Essex County Greenbelt. Turn left along a trail paralleling the river; you'll begin seeing the blue blazes, with a paw print on them, of the Discover Hamilton Trail. Where a footbridge leads right over the river, turn left up a forest road. At a long, wide meadow, turn right and continue onto a forest road back to the park headquarters.

User Groups

Hikers, bikers, dogs, horses, skiers, and snowshoers. Dogs must be leashed. No wheelchair facilities. Hunting is allowed in season.

Access and Fees

A daily parking fee of $5 is collected from mid-May to mid-October.

Maps

A free trail map is available at the park headquarters or at the Massachusetts Division of State Parks and Recreation website.

Directions

From U.S. 1 in Topsfield, turn east onto Ipswich Road (at a traffic light). Drive 1.2 miles and turn right onto Asbury Street. The state park entrance is on the left, a short distance down the road. Park in a dirt area just before the state park headquarters.

Contact

Bradley Palmer State Park, Asbury Street, Topsfield, MA 01983, 978/887-5931. Massachusetts Division of State Parks and Recreation, 251 Causeway Street, Suite 600, Boston, MA 02114-2104, 617/626-1250, website: www.state.ma.us/dem/forparks.htm.

5 HALIBUT POINT

in Halibut Point State Park and Reservation in Rockport

Total distance: 0.5 miles round-trip   **Hiking time:** 0.5 hour

Difficulty: 1   **Rating:** 8

Halibut Point consists of Halibut Point Reservation and Halibut Point State Park and is jointly managed by The Trustees of Reservations and the state. The state park surrounds the site of the former Babson Farm granite quarry, which operated for nearly a century and is now filled with water, creating a small pond ringed by the sheer cliffs of the quarry walls. I visited late one spring day, when the low sun was highlighting thin clouds, creating beautiful reflections in the pond. The park's name derives from "Haul About Point," the name given to the 50-foot granite cliff at the ocean's edge by sailors tacking around the point to approach Cape Ann.

From the parking lot, cross Gott Avenue, following signs to the park entrance. A short trail through trees leads to the quarry. The park headquarters is to the left. Take the trail that goes around the quarry to the right. You pass a mooring stone—an enormous granite slab sunk underwater that anchors an oak post used as a mooring for fishermen's boats. Turn onto a trail branching to the right, toward the ocean, to reach The Trustees of Reservations property. The shore here is very rocky, an extremely wild place when the surf is high; be sure not to get too close to the water because the rip-

Halibut Point

tide is powerful. Walk to the left along the shore and then follow a trail back up toward the quarry. To return, walk around the quarry to the left, which takes you back to the entrance trail.

User Groups

Hikers and dogs. Dogs must be leashed. No wheelchair facilities. This trail very rarely receives enough snow for skis or snowshoes, and is not suitable for bikes or horses. Hunting is prohibited.

Access and Fees

Halibut Point is open to the public from sunrise to sunset year-round. From mid-May to mid-October, hours are 8 A.M.–8 P.M. and a $2 fee is charged for parking. For the rest of the year, the park is open at no charge during the daylight hours. The Trustees of Reservations members park for free.

Maps

A free trail map is available at the park. A map is also available at the Massachusetts Division of State Parks and Recreation website.

Directions

From the junction of Routes 128 and 127, follow Route 127 north (on Eastern Avenue) toward Rockport. After three miles, turn left onto Railroad Avenue, which is still Route 127. After another 2.4 miles, turn right onto Gott Avenue. The parking lot is on the right a short distance up the road.

Contact

Halibut Point State Park, Gott Avenue, Rockport, MA 01966, 978/546-2997. The Trustees of Reservations, Long Hill, 572 Essex Street, Beverly, MA 01915-1530, 978/921-1944, website: www.thetrustees.org. Massachusetts Division of State Parks and Recreation, 251 Causeway Street, Suite 600, Boston, MA 02114-2104, 617/626-1250, website: www.state.ma.us/dem/forparks.htm.

6 DOGTOWN
in Gloucester and Rockport

Total distance: 8.8 miles round-trip   **Hiking time:** 5 hours

Difficulty: 7   **Rating:** 7

This patch of untamed woods in the heart of Cape Ann has become a favorite among local hikers and mountain bikers for its rugged trails, glacial-erratic boulders scattered through the forest, and the legacy of a wealthy financier named Roger Babson. Babson hired stonecutters to carve sayings into rocks here like "Get a Job" and "Never Try Never Win." The old woods roads along this hike carry names but are not maintained thoroughfares for motor vehicles; many are very difficult to negotiate, even for experienced mountain bikers. This rolling, nearly nine-mile route through Dogtown could take five hours hiking, three to four hours on bikes.

From the parking area, go around the gate and follow the rough dirt Dogtown Road for 1.2 miles, passing old cellar holes on the left, to Dogtown Square, a junction of trails where a rock is inscribed "D.T. SQ." From Dogtown Square, turn right onto a rock-strewn dirt road and follow it for 0.1 mile, then turn right again (where the red blazes of the Beaver Dam Trail branch left) onto the Tent Rock Trail, sometimes called the Boulder Trail. It continues for a mile to Babson Reservoir, along the way passing the large boulders inscribed with messages such as "Truth," "Industry," and "Help Mother." From the view of the reservoir, the trail turns left, crosses railroad tracks, and reaches the rough dirt Old Rockport Road behind Blackburn Industrial Park, 1.4 miles from Dogtown Square. Turn left and follow the road 1.2 miles to the Babson Museum on Eastern Avenue/Route 127. Behind the museum, turn left onto the red-blazed Beaver Dam Trail. Crossing the railroad tracks, then a brook four times, the trail passes over a small hill, takes a sharp right, and reaches Dogtown Square, 1.4 miles from the museum. Turn right onto Wharf Road and follow it 0.4 mile to Common Road. Turn right onto the Whale's Jaw Trail, pass a huge boulder called Peter's Pulpit at about 0.3 mile, and reach the Whale's Jaw, another massive boulder, at

0.8 mile. Backtrack the same way to Dogtown Square and follow Dogtown Road back to the parking area.

User Groups
Hikers, bikers, and dogs. No wheelchair facilities. This trail rarely receives enough snow for skis or snowshoes, and is not suitable for horses. Hunting is permitted in season.

Access and Fees
Parking and access are free.

Maps
A free trail map of Dogtown is available from the Gloucester Chamber of Commerce. For a topographic area map, request Rockport from USGS Map Sales, Federal Center, Box 25286, Denver, CO 80225, 888/ASK-USGS (888/275-8747), website: http://mapping.usgs.gov.

Directions
From the Grant Circle Rotary on Route 128 in Gloucester, take Route 127/Washington Street north for 0.9 mile and turn right onto Reynard Street. Follow Reynard to a left onto Cherry Street. Then turn right onto the access road to Dogtown, 1.5 miles from Grant Circle Rotary. Drive less than a half mile to a parking area and a gate.

Contact
Cape Ann Chamber of Commerce, 33 Commercial Street, Gloucester, MA 01930, 978/283-1601, website: www.capeannvacations.com.

⑦ GREAT MEADOWS NATIONAL WILDLIFE REFUGE

in Concord

Total distance: 2 miles round-trip

Hiking time: 1.5 hours

Difficulty: 1

Rating: 9

Although most visitors here are bird-watchers, even the casual walker can't help but be impressed by the profusion of winged creatures on this 3,000-acre refuge, stretching along 12 miles of the Concord River. From great blue herons and osprey to songbirds and wood ducks, 221 bird species have been observed here. The Dike Trail around the broad wetlands is considered one of the best birding sites in the state. I watched a great blue not 50 feet away slowly stalking a meal across a shallow marsh. Bring binoculars if you have them. Besides birds, animals such as deer, muskrats, foxes, raccoons, cottontail rabbits, and weasels call the refuge home. With all the standing water here, you can bet there are lots of bugs too, especially in spring. Interestingly, relics of human habitation here date back to 5500 B.C.

Before you begin your hike, check out the view from the observation tower beside the parking lot. Then pick up the Dike Trail, to the right of the tower, which traverses the meadows between Upper Pool and Lower Pool. On the other side, the trail reaches the Concord River banks (where canoeists pull ashore to walk the trail). Turn left, following the trail along the

Great Meadows National Wildlife Refuge

Upper Pool about a quarter mile to the refuge boundary, marked by signs. Turn back and follow the trail around the Lower Pool. You can either double back or, where the Lower Pool ends, take the Edge Trail through the woods back to the entrance road. Turn right on the road to return to the parking lot.

Special note: You can canoe the gentle Sudbury and Concord Rivers through the refuge and put ashore here to walk this trail. Depending on how long a day trip you want, put in along either Route 27, Route 117, or Route 62 and take out along Route 225 on the Carlisle/Bedford line.

User Groups
Hikers, dogs, skiers, snowshoers, and wheelchair users. Dogs must be leashed. Bikes, horses, and hunting are prohibited.

Access and Fees
Parking and access are free.

Maps
A map of hiking trails and a number of brochures about Great Meadows, including a list of bird species sighted here, are available at the trailhead. For a topographic area map, request Maynard from USGS Map Sales, Federal Center, Box 25286, Denver, CO 80225, 888/ASK-USGS (888/275-8747), website: http://mapping.usgs.gov.

Directions
From Route 2 (0.9 mile east of Emerson Hospital and one mile West of Route 126), turn right onto Sudbury Road and continue across Route 117 (2.1 miles). At the stop sign (2.4 miles from Route 117), turn left onto Concord Road. Follow it 0.7 mile to Lincoln-Sudbury Regional High School, then turn left onto Lincoln Road. Continue 1.4 miles to the Great Meadows NWR sign. Turn left onto Weir Hill Road and follow signs to visitors center and headquarters.

Contact
Great Meadows National Wildlife Refuge, Refuge Manager, 73 Weir Hill Road, Sudbury, MA 01776, 978/443-4661, website: http://greatmeadows.fws.gov/.

8 CHANDLER HOVEY PARK
in Marblehead

Total distance: 0.2 miles round-trip   **Hiking time:** 0.25 hour

Difficulty: 1   **Rating:** 8

This town park on Marblehead Neck is a postage stamp–sized parcel of public land amid some of the most stately houses on Massachusetts's North Shore. The sea crashes up against a classic New England rocky shoreline, a beautiful place at any time of year, in any weather. I especially like coming out here on a stormy day when no one else is around. There is no trail; from the parking lot, simply wander out onto the rocks.

User Groups
Hikers only. No wheelchair facilities. This trail rarely receives enough snow for skis or snowshoes and is not suitable for bikes or horses. Dogs and hunting are prohibited.

Access and Fees
Parking and access are free.

Maps
No map is necessary for this short walk, but for topographic area maps, request Lynn and Salem from USGS Map Sales, Federal Center, Box 25286, Denver, CO 80225, 888/ASK-USGS (888/275-8747), website: http://mapping.usgs.gov.

Directions
From the junction of Routes 114 and 129 in Marblehead, turn east onto Route 129. Drive one block to where Route 129 turns right and continue straight ahead onto Ocean Avenue. Follow it nearly a mile, passing Devereaux Beach, onto Marblehead Neck. Bear left onto Harbor Avenue and follow it nearly a mile; it merges onto Ocean Avenue again. Continue 0.2 mile, turn left onto Follett Street, and proceed 0.1 mile to the parking lot at the road's end. If the gate is closed, park on the street.

Contact
Marblehead Parks and Recreation Department, 781/631-3350.

9 WALDEN POND

in Walden Pond State Park Reservation in Concord

Total distance: 1.7 miles round-trip

Hiking time: 1 hour

Difficulty: 1

Rating: 7

In 1845, a 27-year-old former schoolteacher named Henry David Thoreau came to Walden Pond to live on 14 acres owned by his friend, Ralph Waldo Emerson. Thoreau built a small one-room cabin and began his "experiment in simplicity," living a sustenance lifestyle on the pond. At the time, much of Concord was already deforested and the land converted to farms, but the woods around Walden Pond had remained untouched because the sandy soil was not very fertile. Two years, two months, and two days later, Thoreau closed up his house and returned to village life in Concord. Emerson sold the cabin to his gardener. (The cabin no longer stands, but a replica can be seen beside the parking lot.) In 1854, Thoreau published *Walden, or Life in the Woods*—still considered a classic of American literature. Ever since, Walden Pond has stood as a symbol of the American conservation movement.

Today, Walden Pond sits in the middle of a small patch of woods within earshot of busy state routes and a railroad line, yet it remains popular with hikers and cross-country skiers, as well as fishermen and canoeists (a boat launch is on the right side of Route 126, just beyond the parking area). Songbirds, Canada geese, and ducks are commonly seen here.

© MICHAEL LANZA

Walden Pond

From the parking lot, cross Route 126 and walk downhill to the pond. From either end of the beach, the Pond Path circles the pond, usually staying just above the shoreline but offering almost constant pond views. It's a wide, mostly flat trail and is easy to ski. A short side trail, marked by a sign along the Pond Path, leads to Thoreau's house site. Stay on the trails—erosion is a problem here.

User Groups
Hikers, skiers, and snowshoers. Wheelchair users can access the beginning of this trail above the beach on Walden Pond. Bikes, dogs, horses, and hunting are prohibited.

Access and Fees
A daily parking fee of $5 is collected year-round. Park officials may close the entrance if the park reaches capacity. The park is open to the public 5 A.M.–sunset; check for the closing time posted in the parking lot.

Maps
A free map and an informational brochure about Walden Pond are available outside the Shop at Walden Pond, next to the park office at the parking lot's south end. The map can also be obtained at the Massachusetts Division of State Parks and Recreation website. For a topographic area map, request Maynard from USGS Map Sales, Federal Center, Box 25286, Denver, CO 80225, 888/ASK-USGS (888/275-8747), website: http://mapping.usgs.gov.

Directions
From the junction of Routes 2 and 126 in Concord, drive south on Route 126 for 0.3 mile to the Walden Pond State Reservation entrance and parking lot on the left.

Contact
Walden Pond State Park Reservation, 915 Walden Street/Route 126, Concord, MA 01742, 978/369-3254. Massachusetts Division of State Parks and Recreation, 251 Causeway Street, Suite 600, Boston, MA 02114-2104, 617/626-1250, website: www.state.ma.us/dem/forparks.htm. The Shop at Walden Pond, 508/287-5477.

10 MINUTEMAN BIKEWAY

in Somerville, Cambridge, Arlington, Lexington,
and Bedford

Total distance: 11 miles round-trip   **Hiking time:** 5.5 hours

Difficulty: 1   **Rating:** 8

This paved bikeway follows a former railroad bed and is popular
with walkers, runners, bicyclists, families, in-line skaters, and—
when there's snow—cross-country skiers. Many people, particularly students, use the bikeway to commute to work and classes.
The bikeway passes mainly through forest in Bedford and Lexington, and through a wetland in Lexington as well. From Arlington
into Cambridge and Somerville, the bikeway becomes increasing-
ly an urban recreation path. It is flat and can be done in sections
of short lengths, which is why this receives an easy difficulty rating despite its 11-mile total length.

User Groups

Hikers, bikers, dogs, and wheelchair users. This trail does not
usually receive enough snow for skis or snowshoes, and is not
suitable for horses. Hunting is prohibited.

Access and Fees

Parking and access are free.

Maps

A brochure and map of the bikeway is available from the Arlington Planning Department. Boston's Bikemap, a detailed bicycling
map of the metropolitan area, which includes the Minuteman
Bikeway, is available for $4.25 from Rubel BikeMaps, P.O. Box
401035, Cambridge, MA 02140, website: www.bikemaps.com, and
from area stores listed at the website. For topographic area maps,
request Boston South, Boston North, and Maynard from USGS
Map Sales, Federal Center, Box 25286, Denver, CO 80225,
888/ASK-USGS (888/275-8747), website: http://mapping.usgs.gov.

Directions

The Minuteman Bikeway can be accessed from numerous points

for walks or rides of virtually any distance. Its endpoints are behind the T station in Davis Square, between Holland Street and Meacham Road in Somerville; and at the junction of Railroad Avenue and Loomis Street in Bedford. Access points include Massachusetts Avenue in Cambridge at Cameron Avenue and Harvey Street, 0.4 mile south of Route 16; the Alewife T station at the junction of Routes 2 and 16; a parking lot on Lake Street in Arlington, just west of the Brooks Avenue traffic lights; Swan Place and Mystic Street in Arlington center, near the junction of Routes 2A and 60 (where the bikeway crosses Massachusetts Avenue); Park Avenue in Arlington (via a stairway), just north of Massachusetts Avenue; Maple Street (Route 2A) in Lexington; Woburn Street in Lexington, just west of Massachusetts Avenue; Hancock and Meriam Streets (at a large parking lot), off Bedford Street (Route 4 and Route 225) and the Lexington Battle Green; and Bedford Street (Route 4 and Route 225) between North Hancock and Revere Streets in Lexington.

Contact
The Friends of the Minuteman Bikeway, website: http://users .rcn.com/hwbingham/lexbike/friends.htm. Rails to Trails Conservancy, 1100 17th Street Northwest, 10th floor, Washington, DC 20036, 202/331-9696, website: www.railtrails.org.

11 MIDDLESEX FELLS SKYLINE TRAIL

in Middlesex Fells Reservation In Medford, Malden,
Winchester, Melrose, and Stoneham

Total distance: 7 miles round-trip　　　**Hiking time:** 4 hours

Difficulty: 7　　　　　　　　　　　　　　**Rating:** 8

This may be the premier hiking circuit in the Fells, a 2,000-acre
piece of woods in an urban wilderness. ("Fells" is a Saxon word
for rocky hills.) You can actually find quiet and solitude along
parts of this trail—although traffic on the interstate can be heard
at times, and the Fells as a whole sees heavy recreational use.
The trail loops around the Winchester Reservoirs, passing
through forest and traversing countless rocky ledges, some with
good views of the Fells and, occasionally, the Boston skyline.
Perhaps the best view is from atop Pine Hill, near the start of
this loop, which overlooks Boston's skyline and the Blue Hills to
the south; climb the stone Wright's Tower on the hill. The white
blazes of the Skyline Trail are generally easy to follow, but it
crosses many other paths and forest roads, which can cause con-
fusion. The trail dries out fairly quickly after the snow melts—it's
a glorious hike on the first warm day of spring. Bikes are prohibited from this trail, and it's not suited to skiing, but there are
many forest roads and trails forming a network through the Fells
that offer good mountain biking and cross-country skiing.

From the parking lot, walk along the right side of Bellevue Pond
and onto a wide forest road at the opposite end of the pond. Look
for the white-blazed trail leading to the right, up Pine Hill. The
loop eventually brings you back to this intersection.

User Groups

Hikers and dogs. Dogs must be leashed. No wheelchair facilities.
This trail rarely receives enough snow for snowshoes, and is not
suitable for horses or skis. Bikes are prohibited from the Skyline
Trail. Mountain biking in groups of five or fewer is permitted on
fire roads and the designated Mountain Bike Loop from mid-April
to mid-December. Mountain biking is not permitted on single-
track (hiking) trails and is prohibited in all parts of the reservation
from January 1 to April 15 to protect trails and fire roads from

erosion damage during this often-muddy season. Hunting is prohibited throughout the Middlesex Fells Reservation.

Access and Fees
Parking and access are free. The reservation is open year-round from sunrise to sunset.

Maps
A trail map of the Middlesex Fells Reservation is available for $5 via mail (with SASE) from The Friends of Middlesex Fells Reservation, and sometimes at Bookends Bookstore, at 559 Main Street, Winchester, 781/721-5933; The Map Shack, 253 North Avenue, Wakefield, 781/213-7989; The Book Oasis, 297 Main Street, Stoneham, 781/438-0077; and Best Sellers Café, 24 High Street, Medford Square, 781/391-7171.

Directions
Take I-93 to Exit 33 in Medford. From the traffic circle, turn onto South Border Road. Drive 0.2 mile and turn into a parking area on the right, at Bellevue Pond.

Contact
Middlesex Fells Reservation, 781/322-2851 or 781/662-5230. Massachusetts Division of Urban Parks and Recreation, Commissioner's Office, 20 Somerset Street, Boston, MA 02108, 617/722-5000, website: www.state.ma.us/mdc/mdc_home. The Friends of the Middlesex Fells Reservation, 4 Woodland Road, Stoneham, MA 02180, 781/662-2340, website: www.fells.org.

12 PAUL DUDLEY WHITE CHARLES RIVER BIKE PATH

in the Charles River Reservation, Boston, Cambridge, and Watertown

Total distance: 14 miles round-trip

Hiking time: 6 hours

Difficulty: 1

Rating: 8

The paved Paul Dudley White Bike Path along both banks of the Charles River teems with activity weekday evenings and weekends: walkers, runners, in-line skaters, bicyclists, skateboarders, people of all ages out getting exercise in the middle of the city. It is easily reached from such colleges as MIT, Boston University, and Harvard, and it accesses riverside attractions like the Esplanade and Hatch Shell. The bike path provides a more convenient, more pleasant, and often faster means of getting around the city than driving or using public transportation. It also has great skyline views of Boston from the Cambridge side. For the 20th anniversary Earth Day concert several years ago, when hundreds of thousands of concertgoers jammed the Esplanade and Storrow Drive was closed to motor vehicles, a friend and I easily biked to the show, then left without getting stuck in the crowds afterward. Some sections of the path are quite wide, others no wider than a pair of bikes; likewise, some stretches see much heavier use than others. Bicycling quickly can be difficult when the path is crowded, and numerous crossings of busy streets necessitate frequent stops. The entire path forms a 14-mile loop between the Museum of Science and Watertown Square and can be traveled in either direction and done in smaller sections, which is why this trail receives such an easy difficulty rating.

User Groups

Hikers, bikers, dogs, and wheelchair users. Dogs must be leashed. This path rarely receives enough snow for skis, and is not suitable for snowshoeing. Horses and hunting are prohibited.

Access and Fees

Parking and access are free.

Maps

Boston's Bikemap, a detailed bicycling map of the metropolitan area, which covers the Paul Dudley White Charles River Bike Path, is available for $4.25 from Rubel BikeMaps, P.O. Box 401035, Cambridge, MA 02140, website: www.bikemaps.com, and from area stores listed at the website. For a topographic area map, request Boston South from USGS Map Sales, Federal Center, Box 25286, Denver, CO 80225, 888/ASK-USGS (888/275-8747), website: http://mapping.usgs.gov.

Directions

The bike path runs for seven miles along both sides of the Charles River, from the Boston Museum of Science on the O'Brien Route/Route 28 to Watertown Square in Watertown (the junction of Routes 16 and 20), forming a 14-mile loop. It is accessible from numerous points in Boston, Cambridge, and Watertown, including the footbridges over Storrow Drive in Boston, although not from the Longfellow and Boston University bridges on the Boston side.

Contact

Massachusetts Division of Urban Parks and Recreation, Commissioner's Office, 20 Somerset Street, Boston, MA 02108, 617/722-5000, website: www.state.ma.us/mdc/mdc_home.

🔢 NOANET WOODLANDS
in Dover

Total distance: 4 miles round-trip

Hiking time: 2 hours

Difficulty: 3

Rating: 8

The 695-acre Noanet Woodlands is a surprisingly quiet and se-cluded-feeling forest patch plunked down in the middle of subur-bia. I suspect it comes as a shock to many first-time hikers of 387-foot Noanet Peak to find that virtually the only sign of civi-lization visible from this rocky knob is the Boston skyline 20 miles away—floating on the horizon like the Emerald City. You have to scan the unbroken forest and rolling hills for a glimpse of another building. And you may hear no other sounds than the breeze and singing of birds.

The yellow-blazed Caryl Trail begins at one end of the park-ing lot. Follow it to Junction 6 (trail junction signs are on trees) and turn left onto an unmarked trail. Pass a trail enter-ing on the right. At the next junction, turn right and then left up a hill. You soon reach the open ledge atop Noanet Peak. After enjoying the view, walk to your right a short distance onto a trail that follows a wooded ridge crest, slowly descend-ing to the Caryl Trail; turn left (you'll almost immediately re-cross the trail leading to Noanet's summit, but do not turn onto it). Follow the Caryl Trail to Junction 18 and walk straight onto the blue-blazed Peabody Trail. Pass ponds and the site of an old mill on the right. (From 1815 to 1840, Noanet Brook powered the Dover Union Iron Company. A flood breached the huge dam at Noanet Falls in 1876. In 1954, then-owner Amelia Peabody rebuilt the dam.) Bear left through Junction 4 and turn right onto the Caryl Trail again, which leads back to the parking lot.

User Groups

Hikers, skiers, snowshoers, and horses. No wheelchair facilities. Bikes are allowed by permit only; the price of the permit is dis-counted for The Trustees of Reservations members. Dogs are prohibited at Caryl Park, but visitors who walk to Noanet Wood-lands can bring their dog. Hunting is prohibited.

Access and Fees

Parking and access are free. Noanet Woodlands is open to the public from sunrise to sunset year-round. A biking permit can be obtained at the Noanet Woodlands ranger station at the Caryl Park entrance on weekends and holidays, or from the Southeast Region office of The Trustees of Reservations.

Maps

A trail map is posted on an information board at the trailhead, and one is available free from The Trustees of Reservations, either at the trailhead or through The Trustees headquarters. Major trail junctions in Noanet are marked with numbered signs that correspond to markings on the map. For topographic area maps, request Boston South, Framingham, Medfield, and Norwood from USGS Map Sales, Federal Center, Box 25286, Denver, CO 80225, 888/ASK-USGS (888/275-8747), website: http://mapping.usgs.gov.

Directions

From I-95/Route 128, take Exit 17 onto Route 135 west. Drive about 0.6 mile and turn left at the traffic lights onto South Street. Drive 0.7 mile and bear left at a fork. After another 0.4 miles, turn left onto Chestnut Street. Cross the Charles River and enter Dover; turn right onto Dedham Street. Two miles past the river, turn left into Caryl Park; the sign is hard to see, but the parking lot is next to tennis courts.

Contact

The Trustees of Reservations Southeast/Cape Cod Regional Office, The Bradley Estate, 2468B Washington Street, Canton, MA 02021-1124, 781/821-2977, website: www.thetrustees.org.

14 WHISTLING CAVE
in Upton State Forest in Upton

Total distance: 3 miles round-trip

Hiking time: 1.5 hours

Difficulty: 3

Rating: 7

Whistling Cave is not a cave but two large boulders, one leaning against the other, with a small passageway beneath them. It's located in an interesting little wooded stream valley littered with such boulders. Trails are well blazed, the forest road intersections are marked by signs, and the state forest has many more miles of both trails and roads. This hike has some hills but is relatively easy.

From the parking lot, head past the gate on a dirt forest road to the junction of Loop Road and Park Road. Bear right on Park Road, passing one blue-blazed trail on the left (which may not appear on the map). Continue up a gentle hill to a pullout on the left. The Whistling Cave Trail, marked by a sign and blazed with blue triangles, begins there. It soon drops over ledges and down a steep embankment, then levels out. You cross a couple of small brooks and then enter the area of boulders. Whistling Cave is right on the trail at this area's far end, shortly after you start up a hillside. Just beyond it, the trail ends at the junction of Middle Road and Loop Road. (To reach Whistling Cave on bikes, horses, or skis, take Loop Road to this intersection, walk or attempt to ski to the boulders, and double back.) You can return on either Loop Road or Middle Road; the former remains a forest road, while the latter eventually narrows to an easy trail marked by blue triangles.

User Groups
Hikers, snowshoers, and dogs. Dogs must be leashed. No wheelchair facilities. Bikes, horses, and skis are prohibited. Hunting is allowed in season.

Access and Fees
Parking and access are free.

Maps
A free map is available at the state forest entrance or at the Massachusetts Division of State Parks and Recreation website.

For a topographic area map, request Milford from USGS Map Sales, Federal Center, Box 25286, Denver, CO 80225, 888/ASK-USGS (888/275-8747), website: http://mapping.usgs.gov.

Directions

From I-495, take Exit 21B for West Main Street, Upton, and drive 3.7 miles south to the junction of High Street, Hopkinton Road, and Westboro Road; there is a pond to the left. (The junction can be reached in the other direction from Route 140 in Upton center by taking North Main Street for 0.5 mile.) Turn north onto Westboro Road, drive two miles, and then turn right at the sign for Upton State Forest. Bear right onto a dirt road and stop at the map box. Continue down that dirt road a short distance to a parking lot at a gate.

Contact

Upton State Forest, 205 Westboro Road, Upton, MA 01568, 508/278-6486. Massachusetts Division of State Parks and Recreation, 251 Causeway Street, Suite 600, Boston, MA 02114-2104, 617/626-1250, website: www.state.ma.us/dem/forparks.htm.

🔟🔟 ROCKY WOODS
in Medfield

Total distance: 2.3 miles round-trip   **Hiking time:** 1.5 hours

Difficulty: 1   **Rating:** 7

This 491-acre patch of woodlands boasts more than 12 miles of cart paths and foot trails and is popular with locals for activities from walking and cross-country skiing to fishing (catch-and-release only). There are many more loop possibilities besides the one described here.

Walk down the entrance road to the Quarry Trail and follow it 0.1 mile along the shore of Chickering Pond. Bear left at Junction 2, continue 0.1 mile, and then continue straight through Junction 3. At Junction 4, 0.5 mile from Junction 3, cross the Harwood Notch Trail diagonally, staying on the Quarry Trail. A quarter mile farther, at Junction 7, turn right on the Ridge Trail and walk 0.7 mile. Bear right at Junction 6, turn left immediately after that at Junction 5, and follow the cart path more than a half mile back to Junction 2. The pond and parking area lie straight ahead.

User Groups

Hikers, bikers, horses, skiers, and snowshoers. No wheelchair facilities. Dogs and hunting are prohibited, although the moratorium on walking dogs may eventually be lifted.

Access and Fees

There's an entrance fee of $3 per person age 12 and older, with The Trustees of Reservations members entering free. The reservation is open daily from sunrise to sunset year-round.

Maps

A free trail map is available from the ranger on duty weekends and holidays. Trail intersections numbered on the map correspond to numbered trail signs. For topographic area maps, request Medfield and Norwood from USGS Map Sales, Federal Center, Box 25286, Denver, CO 80225, 888/ASK-USGS (888/275-8747), website: http://mapping.usgs.gov.

Directions

From I-95/Route 128 in Westwood, take Exit 16B onto Route 109, driving west for 5.7 miles. Take a sharp right onto Hartford Street and continue 0.6 mile to the reservation entrance on the left. Or from the junction of Routes 27 and 109 in Medfield, drive 1.7 miles east on Route 109 and bear left on Hartford Street and park along that street.

Contact

The Trustees of Reservations Southeast/Cape Cod Regional Office, The Bradley Estate, 2468B Washington Street, Canton, MA 02021-1124, 781/821-2977, website: www.thetrustees.org.

16 BLUE HILLS: SKYLINE TRAIL LOOP
in the Blue Hills Reservation in Canton

Total distance: 4.5 miles round-trip   **Hiking time:** 2.5 hours

Difficulty: 5   **Rating:** 8

With 5,800 forest acres spread over 20 hilltops, the Blue Hills
Reservation in Quincy, Braintree, Randolph, Canton, and Milton
comprises the largest tract of open space in Greater Boston. It
hosts a broad diversity of flora and fauna, including the timber
rattlesnake, which you are extremely unlikely to encounter given
the snake's fear of people. The reservation harbors an extensive
network of trails and carriage roads—but be aware that some are
unmarked and confusing, and many are rocky and surprisingly
rugged. At 635 feet, Great Blue Hill, near the reservation's western end, is the park's highest point and probably its most popular hike.

This 4.5-mile loop on the north and south branches of the Skyline Trail passes over Great Blue and four other hills, climbing a
cumulative total of about 1,200 feet. It incorporates several good
views—the best being the panorama from the stone tower on
Great Blue, reached near this hike's end. In fact, while the native
granite tower is less than 50 years old, it symbolizes this high
point's long history. Patriots used Great Blue as a lookout during
the Revolutionary War, lighting beacons up here to warn of any
British attack, and for several hundred years, fires have been lit
on Great Blue to celebrate historic occurrences, beginning with
the repeal of the Stamp Act and including the signing of the De-
claration of Independence.

From the parking lot, walk back toward the Howard Johnson's,
watching for blue blazes that cross the road within 100 feet, and
enter the woods at a granite post inscribed with the words "Skyline Trail." The trail ascends steeply for 0.5 mile, reaching open
ledges and the carriage road just below the summit. Turn right on
the carriage road, where blue blazes are often marked on stones
(which may be covered by snow in winter). Pass the path leading
to the summit (there aren't any views, and the observatory is private property), and within 0.1 mile turn right with the blue blazes
onto a footpath marked by a post inscribed "South Skyline Trail."

It descends ledges with good views of the Boston skyline and Houghton Pond, enters the woods, and, within a mile of Great Blue, reaches wooded Houghton Hill. Descend a short distance to Hillside Street, cross it, turn left, and follow the blue blazes about 150 feet to where the blazes direct you back across the street toward the reservation headquarters (passing a post marked "North Skyline Trail"). Walk up the driveway and left of the headquarters onto a carriage path. In about 75 feet, turn right at a sign onto the North Skyline Trail. In minutes you reach an open ledge on Hancock Hill with a view of Great Blue Hill.

Continuing over Hemenway Hill and Wolcott Hill in the next mile, watch for side paths leading right to views of Boston. The Skyline Trail drops downhill, crosses a carriage path, and then climbs the north side of Great Blue to the stone tower. Climb the stairs to the tower for a sweeping view of woods, city, and ocean. From the tower's observation deck looking west (out over the stone building beside the tower), you may see Mount Wachusett (for hikes, see the Central Massachusetts chapter). Standing on the side of the tower facing Boston, look left: On a clear day, you'll spy Mount Monadnock between two tall radio towers in the distance. Descend the stone tower and turn right on the Skyline Trail, circling around Great Blue, past the posts marking the south and north Skyline Trail branches. Make a left turn at the third Skyline Trail post and descend 0.5 mile to Route 138, where you began this hike.

User Groups
Hikers and dogs. Dogs must be leashed. No wheelchair facilities. This trail is not suitable for skis or snowshoes. Bikes and hunting are prohibited, though bikes are permitted on some other specifically marked trails in the Blue Hills.

Access and Fees
Parking and access are free.

Maps
A trail map of the Blue Hills is available at the reservation headquarters or the Massachusetts Audubon Society Blue Hills Trailside Museum. The *Blue Hills Reservation/Mount Tom/Holyoke Range*

map costs $5.95 in paper from the Appalachian Mountain Club, 800/262-4455, website: www.outdoors.org. For a topographic area map, request Norwood from USGS Map Sales, Federal Center, Box 25286, Denver, CO 80225, 888/ASK-USGS (888/275-8747), website: http://mapping.usgs.gov.

Directions

From I-93, take Exit 2B onto Route 138 north. Continue for nearly a half mile, passing the Howard Johnson's, to a commuter parking lot on the left. The reservation headquarters is at 695 Hillside Street in Milton, reached via the reservation entrance on Route 138, before the Howard Johnson's, or from Randolph Avenue (I-93 Exit 5).

Contact

Blue Hills Reservation Headquarters, 695 Hillside Street, Milton, MA 02186, 617/698-1802, website: www.state.ma.us/mdc/blue.htm. Friends of the Blue Hills, P.O. Box 416, Milton, MA 02186, 781/828-1805, website: www.friendsofthebluehills.org. Massachusetts Audubon Society Blue Hills Trailside Museum, 1904 Canton Avenue/Route 138, Milton, MA 02186, 781/333-0690, website: www.massaudubon.org/Nature_Connection/Sanctuaries/Blue_Hills.

17 BLUE HILLS: RATTLESNAKE AND WAMPATUCK HILLS

in the Blue Hills Reservation in Braintree

Total distance: 2.2 miles round-trip   **Hiking time:** 1.5 hours

Difficulty: 2   **Rating:** 8

While many hikers flock to the west side of the reservation and to Great Blue Hill, the east side of the reservation remains a fairly well-kept secret—and the views from there are arguably better than those from Great Blue Hill. Standing in a warm summer breeze on Rattlesnake Hill one afternoon, gazing out over an expanse of woods to the Boston skyline in the distance, I listened, and listened . . . and realized I couldn't hear any traffic. I heard only the breeze and the singing of birds, despite having left the interstate behind just a half hour earlier and hiking merely 0.5 mile.

From the roadside parking area, follow the Skyline Trail, which quickly ascends a short but steep hillside to a view of the thickly forested, rolling hills of the reservation and the Boston skyline beyond. The trail bends around an old quarry now filled with water, and about a half mile from the road reaches the rocky top of Rattlesnake Hill, with excellent views of the hills and skyline. Wampatuck Hill, with more good views, lies less than a half mile farther. There is a short, rocky scramble along the trail between Rattlesnake and Wampatuck that may be intimidating for some inexperienced hikers. Return the same way.

User Groups

Hikers and dogs. Dogs must be leashed. No wheelchair facilities. This trail is not suitable for skis or snowshoes. Bikes and hunting are prohibited, though bikes are permitted on some other specifically marked trails in the Blue Hills.

Access and Fees

Parking and access are free. This trail is closed 8 P.M.–dawn.

Maps

A trail map of the Blue Hills is available at the reservation headquarters or the Massachusetts Audubon Society Blue Hills Trailside Museum. The *Rhode Island NW–SW/Blue Hills Map* costs $5.95 in waterproof Tyvek or $2.95 paper from the Appalachian Mountain Club, 800/262-4455, website: www.outdoors.org. For a topographic area map, request Norwood from USGS Map Sales, Federal Center, Box 25286, Denver, CO 80225, 888/ASK-USGS (888/275-8747), website: http://mapping.usgs.gov.

Directions

From I-93 in Braintree, take Exit 6 and follow signs to Willard Street. About a mile from I-93, watch for the ice rink on the left. Drive 0.2 mile beyond the rink, turn left on Hayden Street, and then immediately left again on Wampatuck Road. Drive another 0.2 mile and park at the roadside on the right, where a post marks the Skyline Trail. The reservation headquarters is at 695 Hillside Street in Milton, reached via the reservation entrance on Route 138, before the Howard Johnson's, or from Randolph Avenue (I-93 Exit 5).

Contact

Blue Hills Reservation Headquarters, 695 Hillside Street, Milton, MA 02186, 617/698-1802, website: www.state.ma.us/mdc/blue.htm. Friends of the Blue Hills, P.O. Box 416, Milton, MA 02186, 781/828-1805, website: www.friendsofthebluehills.org. Massachusetts Audubon Society Blue Hills Trailside Museum, 1904 Canton Avenue/Route 138, Milton, MA 02186, 781/333-0690, website: www.massaudubon.org/Nature_Connection/Sanctuaries/Blue_Hills.

18 WORLD'S END
in Hingham

Total distance: 2.9 miles round-trip

Difficulty: 2

Hiking time: 1.5 hours

Rating: 8

This 251-acre peninsula in Hingham nearly became a community of 163 homes in the late 1800s, when then-landowner John Brewer hired none other than the famous landscape architect Frederick Law Olmsted to design a landscape of carriage paths lined by English oaks and native hardwoods. That much was accomplished, but the Brewer family continued to farm the land rather than develop it. Today, thanks to The Trustees of Reservations, this string of four low hills rising above Hingham Harbor provides local people with a wonderful recreation area for walking, running, or cross-country skiing. Bird-watchers flock here, particularly in spring and fall, to observe migratory species. From various spots, you'll enjoy views of the Boston skyline, Hingham Harbor, and across the Weir River to Hull. This hike loops around the property's perimeter, but four miles of carriage paths and three miles of foot trails, all interconnected, offer many other possible routes for exploration.

From the entrance, walk straight (northwest) along the flat carriage path for 0.25 mile and then bear left around the west flank of Planter's Hill. A quarter mile past Planter's, cross the narrow land bar between the harbor and river, and turn left onto another carriage road. This follows a 0.5-mile curve around a hillside; turn left at the next junction of carriage paths. After another half mile, bear left again, reaching the land bar 0.25 mile farther. Bear left, continue 0.3 mile, then turn right and walk nearly 0.4 mile back to the entrance.

User Groups
Hikers, dogs, skiers, and snowshoers. Dogs must be leashed. No wheelchair facilities. Horses are allowed by permit. Bikes and hunting are prohibited.

Access and Fees
There is an entrance fee of $4.50 per person age 12 and older,

except for members of The Trustees of Reservations, who enter free. The reservation is open daily 8 A.M.–sunset year-round.

Maps

A map of the carriage paths and trails is available free at the entrance. For a topographic area map, request Hull from USGS Map Sales, Federal Center, Box 25286, Denver, CO 80225, 888/ASK-USGS (888/275-8747), website: http://mapping.usgs.gov.

Directions

From the junction of Routes 228 and 3A, drive north on 3A for 0.6 mile. Turn right on Summer Street, drive 0.3 mile, proceed straight through the traffic lights, and then continue another 0.8 mile to the World's End entrance.

Contact

The Trustees of Reservations Southeast/Cape Cod Regional Office, The Bradley Estate, 2468B Washington Street, Canton, MA 02021-1124, 781/821-2977, website: www.thetrustees.org.

⑲ CARATUNK WILDLIFE REFUGE
in Seekonk

Total distance: 2 miles round-trip   **Hiking time:** 1 hour

Difficulty: 1   **Rating:** 7

Bird-watchers will want to visit here during April and May or from late August to October to catch the migratory birds, but this easy, two-mile walk mostly through woods is a satisfying outing any time of year. There are a few trail options in the refuge, all of them well blazed; this loop, mostly on the blue trail, is the longest, winding through much of the property, past open fields, wetlands, and two small ponds.

From the parking lot, walk to the right of the building, past the information kiosk and along the field's right edge. Soon a short side path loops into the woods to the right, bringing you along a bog, then back out to the field. Walk a short distance farther along the field, then turn right onto the red trail. After passing through a pine grove and skirting the far edge of the same field where you began, turn right onto the yellow trail and then bear left onto the blue trail. At the edge of Muskrat Pond, turn right, staying on blue past Ice Pond, crossing power lines, passing another pond, and continuing through the beech woods and a hemlock stand; you'll pass several trail junctions and loop back to the bog, where you begin backtracking on the blue trail. After crossing the power lines and passing Ice Pond in the other direction, stay on the blue trail past one junction with the yellow trail and then bear left onto the yellow trail at the next junction. Upon reaching the field, turn right on the red trail and follow it around the field back to the refuge office and parking lot.

User Groups
Hikers, skiers, and snowshoers. No wheelchair facilities. Bikes, dogs, horses, and hunting are prohibited.

Access and Fees
A donation of $1 is requested for nonmembers of the Audubon Society. The refuge is open daily, sunrise to sunset. Visitors should stay on trails.

Maps

A map is available at the refuge. For a topographic area map, request Providence from USGS Map Sales, Federal Center, Box 25286, Denver, CO 80225, 888/ASK-USGS (888/275-8747), website: http://mapping.usgs.gov.

Directions

From I-95 in Attleboro, take Exit 2 onto Newport Avenue southbound/Route 1A. Drive 1.8 miles from the interstate, turn left onto Armistice Boulevard/Route 15, and follow it 1.2 miles to its end. Turn right onto Route 152 south, continue 0.6 mile, and then turn left at a church onto Brown Avenue. Proceed 0.8 mile farther to the refuge entrance on the right.

Contact

Caratunk Wildlife Refuge, 301 Brown Avenue, Seekonk, MA 02771, 508/761-8230. The Audubon Society of Rhode Island, 12 Sanderson Road, Smithfield, RI 02917, 401/949-5454, website: www.asri.org.

20 MYLES STANDISH STATE FOREST LOOP
in Carver

Total distance: 11 miles round-trip   **Hiking time:** 6 hours

Difficulty: 8   **Rating:** 7

Myles Standish State Forest sprawls over more than 14,000 acres, making it one of the largest public lands in Massachusetts. A grid work of old woods roads cuts through this pine barrens, along with a hiking trail and a paved bicycle path. This loop from the forest headquarters, which I did one November afternoon on my mountain bike, connects several dirt woods roads, and much of its course is reserved for skiers in winter (who have to watch out for snowmobiles on other roads in Myles Standish). The grid pattern of roads and the signs at many intersections makes navigating through this vast landscape easier than it might be otherwise, but bring a map. Although the terrain is mostly flat, there are slight rises and dips that can make the workout a little harder on a bike or skis. Also, sand traps crop up periodically, spanning the roads, and I found a few of them impossible to pedal across; fortunately, none of them were very big. Distances in this description are estimates based on the map provided by the state.

From the parking lot, head back out onto Cranberry Road, turn right, and then immediately right again past the headquarters building onto paved Lower College Pond Road into the state forest. Within 0.5 mile, bicyclists and skiers can turn left onto the paved bike path, which leads to the dirt Halfway Pond Road; others will continue 0.25 mile on Lower College Pond Road to the Halfway Pond Road intersection. Turn left onto Halfway Pond Road, follow it 0.5 mile to a crossroads, and turn right onto Jessup Road. Continue about 0.7 mile and bear right at a sign reading "Ebeeme Road," which is shown as Jessup Road on the state map. A half mile farther, turn right at a crossroads onto Federal Pond Road. Follow it a mile, crossing the bridle trail, a gas line right-of-way, and Kamesit Way, and then turn right onto Sabbatia Road. Continue a mile and then turn left onto Three Cornered Pond Road. Reaching the paved Lower College Pond Road within 0.25 mile, turn right, then bear left immediately and proceed straight onto the bridle path (don't turn left onto another bridle path branch), marked by a horse symbol. In 0.25 mile, at the next intersection, turn left onto Negas Road, continue 0.5 mile, and then turn left onto paved Upper College Pond Road. Proceed nearly a half mile and turn right onto Three Cornered Pond Road. Three-quarters of a mile farther, turn right again onto Cobb Road and follow it 0.75 mile to its end. Turn right onto Halfway Pond Road, go about 0.2 mile, and then take the first left. In about 0.3 mile, turn left again onto Doctor's Pond Road, go 0.5 mile, and then turn right onto Webster Springs Road. Follow it nearly a mile, crossing paved Circuit Drive, a dirt road, the bike path, and the bridle path before reaching Upper College Pond Road. Turn left, following the paved road nearly a half mile to its end. Turn right on paved Fearing Pond Road and continue 0.5 mile back to the forest headquarters.

User Groups

Hikers, bikers, dogs, skiers, and snowshoers. The paved bike path is wheelchair accessible. Dogs must be leashed. Horses are prohibited. Hunting is allowed in season.

Access and Fees

A daily parking fee of $5 is collected from mid-May to mid-October.

Maps

A free, basic trail map of Myles Standish State Forest is available at the state forest headquarters or at the Massachusetts Division of State Parks and Recreation website. For topographic area maps, request Plymouth and Wareham from USGS Map Sales, Federal Center, Box 25286, Denver, CO 80225, 888/ASK-USGS (888/275-8747), website: http://mapping.usgs.gov.

Directions

From I-495, take Exit 2 on the Middleborough-Wareham line onto Route 58 north. Drive 2.5 miles to where Route 58 turns left, but continue straight ahead, following signs for the state forest. Proceed another 0.8 mile, turn right onto Cranberry Road, and then drive 2.8 miles to the state forest headquarters and a parking lot on the left.

Contact

Myles Standish State Forest, Cranberry Road, P.O. Box 66, South Carver, MA 02366, 508/866-2526. Massachusetts Division of State Parks and Recreation, 251 Causeway Street, Suite 600, Boston, MA 02114-2104, 617/626-1250, website: www.state.ma.us/dem/forparks.htm.

21 PROVINCE LANDS TRAIL
in the Cape Cod National Seashore in Provincetown

Total distance: 6 miles round-trip

Hiking time: 3 hours

Difficulty: 6

Rating: 8

This paved path is popular with bikers, hikers, runners, in-line skaters, and others, and it's good for wheelchairs, too. The paved bikeway makes a circuitous loop through forest, past ponds, and over sprawling sand dunes—it may be the most interesting bike path I've ever pedaled. Be sure to take the spur path 0.5 mile out to Race Point (included in the mileage), which is near the very tip of Massachusetts and a great place for whale-watching during the seasonal migrations, when the whales often swim close to shore. Heed the center dividing line on this path, especially around its many blind corners. Pick up the bike path from the Beech Forest parking lot; the loop returns here.

User Groups

Hikers, bikers, dogs, and wheelchair users. Dogs must be leashed. This trail rarely receives enough snow for skis or snowshoes. Horses and hunting are prohibited.

Access and Fees

Parking and access are free. Trails are closed to the public midnight–6 A.M. The Province Lands Visitor Center on Race Point Road is open daily 9 A.M.–4:30 P.M.

Maps

A guide to national seashore bike trails is available at the Province Lands and Salt Pond Visitor Centers in Eastham. The *Cape Cod & North Shore Bicycle Map,* a detailed map of roads and bike paths on Cape Cod and the Islands and Cape Ann and the North Shore, is available for $4.25 from Rubel BikeMaps, P.O. Box 401035, Cambridge, MA 02140, website: www.bikemaps.com, and from area stores listed at the website. The waterproof/tearproof *Cape Cod National Seashore Map 250* costs $9.95 from Trails Illustrated, 800/962-1643, website: http://maps.national geographic.com/trails/. For a topographic area map, request

Provincetown from USGS Map Sales, Federal Center, Box 25286, Denver, CO 80225, 888/ASK-USGS (888/275-8747), website: http://mapping.usgs.gov.

Directions
Drive U.S. 6 east to Provincetown. At the traffic lights on U.S. 6, turn right onto Race Point Road. Continue to the Beech Forest parking area on the left; the Province Lands Visitor Center is a short distance farther on the right.

Contact
Cape Cod National Seashore, 99 Marconi Station Site Road, Wellfleet, MA 02667, 508/349-3785, website: www.nps.gov/caco/index.htm. Salt Pond Visitor Center (corner of Nauset Road and Route 6, Eastham), 508/255-3421. Province Lands Visitor Center (on Race Point Road, off Route 6, at the northern end of Cape Cod National Seashore and approximately one mile from Provincetown), 508/487-1256.

22 GREAT ISLAND TRAIL

in the Cape Cod National Seashore in Wellfleet

Total distance: 6 miles round-trip **Hiking time:** 3.5 hours

Difficulty: 6 **Rating:** 10

A friend and I took this hike in late afternoon on a warm spring day as the sinking sun ignited the dunes a vivid yellow that contrasted sharply with the cobalt sky. We watched dozens of tiny crabs scatter from us in a wave of motion that for an instant made me think the sand was inexplicably sliding away. We watched high, thin cirrus clouds create a rainbow halo around the sun. We saw no one else in three hours on this trail—except a lone sea kayaker paddling the glassy waters of the bay far offshore. The beach here is a great place to watch the sun set over Cape Cod Bay.

From the parking lot, the trail enters the woods, following a wide forest road. An optional side loop (adding two miles to the hike) leads to the Tavern Site, so named because fragments of a

© MICHAEL LANZA

a hiker on the Great Island Trail, Cape Cod National Seashore

17th-century tavern were excavated there; nothing remains today, however. The main trail leads over Great Beach Hill—which has no views—and out to the grasslands separating the beach from the forest. Follow that old road around to Jeremy Point overlook, where the dunes end abruptly and you reach the beach on Cape Cod Bay. At low tide, the long spit out to Jeremy Point may be walkable, but be aware that it disappears under the ocean when the tide rises. Return the way you came.

User Groups

Hikers only. No wheelchair facilities. This trail rarely receives enough snow for skis or snowshoes. Bikes, dogs, horses, and hunting are prohibited.

Access and Fees

Parking and access are free. Trails are closed to the public midnight–6 A.M. The Salt Pond Visitor Center is open daily 9 A.M.–4:30 P.M.

Maps

An information board is at the trailhead, and trail information is available at the Salt Pond Visitor Center. The *Cape Cod & North Shore Bicycle Map,* a detailed map of roads and bike paths on Cape Cod and the Islands and Cape Ann and the North Shore, is available for $4.25 from Rubel BikeMaps, P.O. Box 401035, Cambridge, MA 02140, 617/776-6567, website: www.bikemaps.com, and from area stores listed at the website. The waterproof/tearproof *Cape Cod National Seashore Map 250* costs $9.95 from Trails Illustrated, 800/962-1643, website: http://maps.nationalgeographic .com/trails/. For a topographic area map, request Wellfleet from USGS Map Sales, Federal Center, Box 25286, Denver, CO 80225, 888/ASK-USGS (888/275-8747), website: http://mapping.usgs.gov.

Directions

From the Salt Pond Visitor Center at the Doane Road Exit in Eastham, drive U.S. 6 east for 8.2 miles. Turn left at the sign for Wellfleet Center and Harbor. Drive 0.4 mile and turn left at the sign for Blue Harbor. In another 0.6 mile you reach the marina; turn right, following the road (with the water on your left) for 2.5 miles to the Great Island parking lot on the left.

Contact

Cape Cod National Seashore, 99 Marconi Station Site Road, Wellfleet, MA 02667, 508/349-3785, website: www.nps.gov/ caco/index.htm. Salt Pond Visitor Center (corner of Nauset Road and Route 6, Eastham), 508/255-3421. Province Lands Visitor Center, 508/487-1256.

23 ATLANTIC WHITE CEDAR SWAMP

in the Cape Cod National Seashore in South Wellfleet

Total distance: 1 mile round-trip   **Hiking time:** 0.75 hour

Difficulty: 1   **Rating:** 10

I consider this one of the highlights of the national seashore—and almost as much for the site's historic significance as for this short but uniquely beautiful swamp trail. It was from this spot, on January 18, 1903, that the Italian Guglielmo Marconi transmitted a 48-word message to England and received an immediate reply— the first two-way transoceanic communication and first wireless telegram between America and Europe. The four huge towers that once stood here are long gone; in fact, more than half the land where they stood has since eroded into the sea. Considering the way the ocean and wind continually batter this narrowest section of Cape Cod—the peninsula is barely a mile across here—one has to wonder how many years will elapse before the sea cuts the outer cape off completely from the mainland.

The Atlantic White Cedar Swamp Trail begins among stunted oak and pine trees. But as you descend at a very gentle grade, the trees grow taller—they are more protected from the harsh ocean climate in this hollow of sorts. Pitch pine, black and white oak, golden beach-heather, and broom crowberry thrive here, though many are still twisted in the manner characteristic of a place buffeted by almost constant winds. A

Kristine Karlson hikes the boardwalk in Atlantic White Cedar Swamp.

boardwalk winds through the swamp—an eerie depression formed, like other kettles on the cape, by a melting glacial ice block. The swamp's peat floor reaches down 24 feet. Cedars crowd in on the boardwalk, some leaning over it, creating an almost overwhelming sense of intimacy in this odd little forest. The trail emerges abruptly from the swamp onto an old sand road that leads back to the parking lot.

User Groups

Hikers only. The Marconi station is wheelchair accessible. This trail rarely receives enough snow for skis or snowshoes. Bikes, dogs, horses, and hunting are prohibited.

Access and Fees

Parking and access are free. Trails are closed to the public midnight–6 A.M. The Salt Pond Visitor Center is open daily 9 A.M.–4:30 P.M.

Maps

A trail guide is available at the trailhead. Maps and information about the national seashore are available at the Salt Pond Visitor Center. The *Cape Cod & North Shore Bicycle Map,* a detailed map of roads and bike paths on Cape Cod and the Islands and Cape Ann and the North Shore, is available for $4.25 from Rubel BikeMaps, P.O. Box 401035, Cambridge, MA 02140, website: www.bikemaps.com, and from area stores listed at the website. The waterproof/tearproof *Cape Cod National Seashore Map 250* costs $9.95 from Trails Illustrated, 800/962-1643, website: http://maps.nationalgeographic.com/trails/. For a topographic area map, request Wellfleet from USGS Map Sales, Federal Center, Box 25286, Denver, CO 80225, 888/ASK-USGS (888/275-8747), website: http://mapping.usgs.gov.

Directions

Drive U.S. 6 east to Eastham. Five miles beyond the Doane Road exit for the Salt Pond Visitor Center, turn right at signs for the Marconi station and continue to the parking lot. The Marconi station, which has historical displays, is between the lot and the beach. The trail begins at the parking lot.

Contact

Cape Cod National Seashore, 99 Marconi Station Site Road, Wellfleet, MA 02667, 508/349-3785, website: www.nps.gov/caco/index.htm. Salt Pond Visitor Center (corner of Nauset Road and Route 6, Eastham), 508/255-3421. Province Lands Visitor Center, 508/487-1256.

24 NAUSET MARSH

in the Cape Cod National Seashore in Eastham

Total distance: 1.2 miles round-trip   **Hiking time:** 0.75 hour

Difficulty: 1   **Rating:** 7

This easy-to-follow trail has numerous interpretive signs with information about its abundant flora and a good view of Nauset Marsh. From the visitors center parking lot, start out on the Buttonbush Trail for the Blind, which leads shortly to the Nauset Marsh Trail. The Marsh Trail passes through pitch pine, black cherry, and eastern red cedar trees, then follows the edge of Salt Pond. (The pond was created when a glacier receded and left behind enormous salt blocks, which eventually melted, leaving kettle ponds such as this one in their wake. The ocean later broke through a land barrier to infiltrate Salt Pond.) The trail then turns away from the channel connecting pond to ocean and enters a forest of honeysuckle and cedar. It passes an open overlook above Nauset Marsh, which at one time was navigable. After entering a forest of red cedar and bayberry, the trail passes a side path leading nearly a mile to a good view of the marsh at a spot marked by the Doane Memorial, a plaque paying tribute to a family that once owned land here. The loop culminates near the visitors center parking lot.

User Groups

Hikers only. No wheelchair facilities. This trail rarely receives enough snow for skis or snowshoes. Bikes, dogs, horses, and hunting are prohibited.

Access and Fees

Parking and access are free. Trails are closed to the public midnight–6 A.M. The Salt Pond Visitor Center is open daily 9 A.M.–4:30 P.M.

Maps

A trail guide is available in a box at the trailhead, and maps and information about the national seashore are available in the visitors center. The *Cape Cod & North Shore Bicycle Map,* a detailed map of roads and bike paths on Cape Cod and the Islands and Cape Ann and the North Shore, is available for $4.25 from Rubel BikeMaps, P.O. Box 401035, Cambridge, MA 02140, website: www.bikemaps.com, and from area stores listed at the website. The waterproof/tearproof *Cape Cod National Seashore Map 250* costs $9.95 from Trails Illustrated, 800/962-1643, website: http://maps.nationalgeographic.com/trails/. For a topographic area map, request Orleans from USGS Map Sales, Federal Center, Box 25286, Denver, CO 80225, 888/ASK-USGS (888/275-8747), website: http://mapping.usgs.gov.

Directions

Drive U.S. 6 east to Eastham. Take the exit for Doane Road, following signs for national seashore information to the Salt Pond Visitor Center.

Contact

Cape Cod National Seashore, 99 Marconi Station Site Road, Wellfleet, MA 02667, 508/349-3785, website: www.nps.gov/caco/index.htm. Salt Pond Visitor Center (corner of Nauset Road and Route 6, Eastham), 508/255-3421. Province Lands Visitor Center, 508/487-1256.

25 CAPE COD RAIL TRAIL

in Dennis, Harwich, Brewster, Orleans, Eastham, and Wellfleet

Total distance: 25 miles one-way

Hiking time: 12 hours

Difficulty: 1

Rating: 7

Following a former railroad bed, the paved Cape Cod Rail Trail extends for 25 miles from Route 134 in South Dennis to Lecount Hollow Road in South Wellfleet, near the Cape Cod National Seashore's Marconi Visitor Center, making for about a two-hour bike ride. The mostly flat, paved trail crosses cranberry bogs, forests, and several roads, providing numerous access and egress points, including at the entrance to Nickerson State Park on Route 6A in Brewster, and at Locust Road in Eastham, which is off U.S. 6 near the Cape Cod National Seashore's Salt Pond Visitor Center on Doane Road. The trail passes through Nickerson, which has its own hiking trail system and a bike path, and it connects with bike paths at the national seashore. The rail trail is very much a citizen's path—every time I've biked on it, it has been busy with cyclists, in-line skaters, walkers, adults, and children. As such, it can be difficult to bike at a fast pace, but it's a scenic and safe outing for a family. You can do sections of varying length rather than the entire 25-mile distance, which is why this receives such an easy difficulty rating.

User Groups

Hikers, bikers, dogs, horses, and wheelchairs users. Dogs must be leashed. This trail rarely receives enough snow for skis or snowshoes. Hunting is prohibited.

Access and Fees

Parking and access are free.

Maps

The *Cape Cod & North Shore Bicycle Map,* a detailed map of roads and bike paths on Cape Cod and the Islands and Cape Ann and the North Shore, is available for $4.25 from Rubel BikeMaps, P.O. Box 401035, Cambridge, MA 02140, website: www.bike

maps.com, and from area stores listed at the website. Or get the waterproof *Cape Cod National Seashore Map 250* for $9.95 from Trails Illustrated, 800/962-1643, website: http://maps.nationalgeographic.com/trails/. For topographic area maps, request Dennis, Harwich, and Orleans from USGS Map Sales, Federal Center, Box 25286, Denver, CO 80225, 888/ASK-USGS (888/275-8747), website: http://mapping.usgs.gov.

Directions
To reach the trail's western end, from U.S. 6 in Dennis, take Exit 9 onto Route 134 south. Proceed through two traffic signals to a large parking lot on the left for the Cape Cod Rail Trail. The eastern terminus is at Lecount Hollow Road in South Wellfleet, near the Cape Cod National Seashore's Marconi Visitor Center and off U.S. 6. The trail can be accessed at numerous points along its path.

Contact
Cape Cod Rail Trail/Nickerson State Park, P.O. Box 787, Brewster, MA 02631, 508/896-3491, website: www.state.ma.us/dem/parks/ccrt.htm. Massachusetts Division of Forests and Parks, 100 Cambridge Street, 19th Floor, Boston, MA 02202, 800/831-0569 (in-state only) or 617/626-1250 ext. 1451, website: www.state.ma.us/dem/forparks.htm. Rails to Trails Conservancy, 1100 17th Street NW, 10th floor, Washington, DC 20036, 202/331-9696, website: www.railtrails.org.

26 AQUINNAH
in Aquinnah on Martha's Vineyard

Total distance: 3 miles round-trip   **Hiking time:** 1.5 hours

Difficulty: 2   **Rating:** 9

The vibrant pastels of the clay cliffs at Aquinnah, the western-most point of Martha's Vineyard island, are an eye-catching attraction at any time of day, but particularly striking at sunset, when the sun's low, long rays bring out the layered browns, yellows, reds, whites, and deep grays. This hike is an easy walk along Moshup Beach and is popular with tourists. From the parking lot, follow the sandy trail, sometimes crossing a boardwalk, which parallels Moshup Road. Within minutes you are on the beach; turn right and follow the beach to the cliffs. At high tide, you may have difficulty walking to the far end of the cliffs. Head back the way you came.

User Groups
Hikers only. No wheelchair facilities. This trail rarely receives enough snow for skis or snowshoes, and is not suitable for bikes or horses. Dogs and hunting are prohibited.

Access and Fees
A parking fee of $5 per hour, or $15 maximum for a day, is charged from Memorial Day weekend to mid-October, although cyclists, walkers, or anyone not parking a vehicle can access the beach free. Three seasonal ferry services make regular trips, from May to October, to Vineyard Haven or Oak Bluffs from Falmouth, 508/548-4800, and Hyannis, 508/778-2600, on Cape Cod as well as from New Bedford, MA, 508/997-1688. The Steamship Authority, 508/477-8600, carries vehicles and passengers from Woods Hole on Cape Cod to Vineyard Haven year-round and Woods Hole to Oak Bluffs from May 15 to October 15.

Maps
Although no map is needed for this hike, for a topographic area map, request Squibnocket from USGS Map Sales, Federal Cen-

ter, Box 25286, Denver, CO 80225, 888/ASK-USGS (888/275-8747), website. http://mapping.usgs.gov

Directions
The cliffs at Aquinnah are on Moshup Beach at the western tip of Martha's Vineyard, in the town of Aquinnah, and at the end of the State Road, which crosses the island from Vineyard Haven. Ferry services make regular trips to Vineyard Haven and Oak Bluffs from Falmouth and Hyannis on Cape Cod, as well as from New Bedford, MA (see Access and Fees for additional ferry information above).

Contact
Aquinnah Town Hall, 65 State Road, Aquinnah, MA 02535, 508/645-2300. Martha's Vineyard Chamber of Commerce, P.O. Box 1698, Vineyard Haven, MA 02568, 508/693-0085, website: www.mvy.com/islandinfo/townAquinnah.html.

© KINDRA CLINEFF/DCR

Resources

Public Lands Agencies

**Blue Hills Reservation
Headquarters**
695 Hillside Street
Milton, MA 02186
617/698-1802
website: www.state.ma.us/
mdc/blue.htm

Cape Cod National Seashore
99 Marconi Station Site Road
Wellfleet, MA 02667
508/349-3785, fax 508/349-9052
website: www.nps.gov/caco/
index.htm
also: Salt Pond Visitor Center
508/255-3421
also: Province Lands Visitor Center
508/487-1256

**Great Meadows National
Wildlife Refuge**
73 Weir Hill Road
Sudbury, MA 01776
978/443-4661
website: http://greatmeadows
.fws.gov/

**Massachusetts Division of State
Parks and Recreation**
251 Causeway Street, Suite 600
Boston, MA 02114-2104
617/626-1250, fax 617/626-1449
website: www.state.ma.us/dem/
forparks.htm

**Parker River National
Wildlife Refuge**
6 Plum Island Turnpike
Newburyport, MA 01950
978/465-5753, 800/877-8339 for
the hearing impaired
website: http://parkerriver
.fws.gov/

Other Land Managers

The Trustees of Reservations
Long Hill
572 Essex Street
Beverly, MA 01915-1530
978/921-1944
website: www.thetrustees.org

Map Sources

DeLorme Publishing Company
800/253-5081
website: www.DeLorme.com

New England Cartographics
413/549-4124 or toll-free
888/995-6277
website: www.necarto
graphics.com

Rubel BikeMaps
P.O. Box 401035
Cambridge, MA 02140
website: www.bikemaps.com

Trails Illustrated
800/962-1643
website: http://maps.national
geographic.com/trails

United States Geological Survey
Information Services
Box 25286
Denver, CO 80225
888/ASK-USGS (888/275-8747),
fax 303/202-4693
website: http://mapping.usgs.gov

Trail Clubs and Organizations

Appalachian Mountain Club
5 Joy Street
Boston, MA 02108
617/523-0655
website: www.outdoors.org

Appalachian Trail Conference
799 Washington Street
P.O. Box 807
Harpers Ferry, WV 25425-0807
304/535-6331
website: www.appalachiantrail.org

Friends of the Blue Hills
P.O. Box 416
Milton, MA 02186
781/828-1805
website: www.friendsofthe
bluehills.org

**The Friends of the Middlesex
Fells Reservation**
4 Woodland Road
Stoneham, MA 02180
781/662-2340
website: www.fells.org

Friends of the Wapack
Box 115
West Peterborough, NH 03468
website: www.wapack.org

Acknowledgments

I want to thank the many people who accompanied me on these trails, in particular my wife and hiking partner, Penny Beach. My parents, Henry and Joanne Lanza, deserve recognition—both for putting up with a son who has shown up at their door a few times since they first got rid of him, and for being good hiking partners. I also want to thank my editors and the rest of the very talented staff at Avalon Travel Publishing.

While I have personally walked every hike described in this book—some of them many times—updating a volume as comprehensive as this one cannot possibly be accomplished without the assistance of many people. To that end, I relied on friends, acquaintances, people active with hiking and conservation groups, and managers of public lands and private reserves to do some on-the-ground "scouting" of trails and send me current reports on the hikes in this book. Much deep appreciation goes out to: Joe Albee, Mike and Rick Baron, Annette Ermini, Jim Ermini, Mark Fenton, Anna Garofalo, Marco Garofalo, Mike Hannigan, Joe Kuzneski, Brittany Lanza, Cassidy Lanza, Julie Lanza, Kaylee Lanza, Nicholas Lanza, Stephen Lanza, Diane Mailloux, Brion O'Connor, Rod Venterea, and Matt Walsh.

There were also many helpful people at various organizations and public agencies, including: Appalachian Mountain Club; Appalachian Trail Conference; Cape Cod National Seashore; Friends of the Blue Hills; Friends of the Middlesex Fells; Friends of the Wapack; Massachusetts Audubon Society; Massachusetts Division of State Parks and Recreation; Midstate Trail Committee; Mount Greylock State Reservation; New England Cartographics; Rubel BikeMaps; Trails Illustrated; Trustees of Reservations; Williams Outing Club.

Index

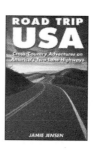